THE TOWNS

THE BEGINNING

The first TOWN Flotilla entering Plymouth Sound 28.9.40 to commence refit for British service. DD 134, to become HMS CHELSEA, follows her sister ships; in the background the French battleship PARIS lies to her moorings at the entrance to the Hamoaze. The Censor has marked the American pennant (pendant) number for deletion on pictures to be released to the public

courtesy Imperial War Museum

THE TOWNS

A history of the fifty destroyers transferred from the United States to Great Britain in 1940

Arnold Hague

U.S. Navy flush deckers laid up in the 1930s. Believed taken on the Pacific Coast, there are some 40 plus ships in this one berth. Clearly visible is the forward hatch to the messdecks, the forward 4" gun with the shields removed and stowed against the bridge. The two nearest ships have the 3"/23 cal fitted between the 4" gun and the bridge, indicating an early building date   *USN*

Published in 1988 by the World Ship Society,
28 Natland Road, Kendal LA9 7LT, England

ISBN 0 905617 48 7

Companion Volume: THE HUNTS: John English

Contents

Cover: H.M.S. RIPLEY

ACKNOWLEDGEMENTS

In the preparation of this book a great deal of assistance has been received from many people, principally but not entirely members of the Society. While it would be pleasant to record all names, space does not permit. However, there are those whose contribution has been so large that they must be mentioned; in photographs (both supply and advice) Ken Macpherson of Toronto and Richard Osborne; my colleague of many years John Burgess, also of Toronto, whose voluminous records have provided so much information, Ian Buxton and Michael Crowdy who so patiently read and re-read the typescript and pointed out the errors for me to correct, my friends in the Naval Historical Library and Branch, Alan Francis, Mac McAloon and Paul Melton who provided so much information. Finally, the Head of that Branch, David Brown, whose pungent witticism caused me to produce this manuscript; it is unfortunately unrepeatable but it would stimulate many of us who accumulate knowledge and hesitate to make proper use of it. Thank you all.

The opinions, and errors, contained in this book are entirely those of its author although every effort has been taken to ensure both accuracy and a balanced view.

A. H.

PHOTOGRAPHIC ACKNOWLEDGEMENTS

The majority of the illustrations are taken from the author's collection accumulated over many years, from the former Admiralty archive: these are credited "Admiralty". Illustrations from the National Maritime Museum and the Imperial War Museum are attributed to their source; other photographs are from private sources and quote the name of the owner.

NMM and IWM photographs are available from the Photographic Departments of the Museums; such of the Admiralty photographs which have survived the passage of time and for which there are negatives, may also be available from the Imperial War Museum as the Admiralty archive no longer exists. Enquirers are recommended to approach the IWM which has prepared an excellent descriptive list of the available TOWN photographs. A copy will be supplied on receipt of a request and the appropriate s.a.e.

My thanks to all, both official and private, but particularly David Hodges, of the NMM, Paul Kemp of the IWM and K Macpherson of Canada.

CENSORS MARKINGS

In the frontispiece, the Censor has marked the American pennant (pendant) number for deletion on pictures to be released to the public. Pennant numbers, where absent from pictures in this book, will generally have been removed on the instructions of the Censor and their absence will give the clue that other details of interest to the enemy may also be missing. Backgrounds, too, can be changed so that the location cannot be identified.

A HISTORY OF THE TOWN CLASS DESTROYERS

The following is a history of the fifty ships of the TOWN class, acquired from the United States in late 1940, so far as it relates to their post transfer service, together with a short account of the original design, and the events leading to transfer. There is no intent to tell the story in 'human' terms, such is left for better writers with personal experience of the times; it is a strictly factual account of the service lives of the ships.

The concept of the text dates back to the first sight by the writer of an Admiralty produced volume presented to each of the American towns for which the ships are named. That volume had been very hurriedly produced in the late 1940s; so hurriedly in fact that less than half the ships were illustrated. Copies of the book are now publicly available in the Imperial War Museum and the Naval Historical Library. As a beginning, therefore, the task of collecting an illustration of each ship commenced.

The work was, apparently, completed in December 1985 with the acquisition of a photograph of ST MARYS. Regrettably, this particular photograph has since proved to be a fake and the quality of some other illustrations is far below that desired, but they have been included rather than fail to illustrate a ship. They include at least two shots apparently taken illicitly in wartime by Canadian ratings, two from the Naval Museum in Leningrad, two wartime German views (one well known and one very rare) and a photograph of a Dutch manned TOWN, obtained initially from a Polish source.

In production of the text, particularly relating to individual summaries of service, much use has been made of movements painstakingly transcribed over the years by a Canadian colleague. Fortunately, the recent discovery of the originals in store in London eased the final task. Comment on the ships' performance etc, has come from reports filed in the Public Record Office at Kew, and also from letters from former Officers.

The following sections will, it is hoped, explain the origins of the ships, the events leading to their acquisition, subsequent alterations in British service with tabular lists of pennant numbers, renamings, and, finally, an individual entry for each vessel detailing its wartime service and ultimate disposal, together with at least one illustration with an explanatory caption.

ORIGINAL CONCEPT AND CONSTRUCTION

The majority of the world's principal navies expanded prodigiously during the period 1914-18, none more so than the United States Navy. Unlike most, it did so from a major (and uninterrupted) industrial base, with public, political and Service will in concert to build the world's greatest Fleet.

Apart from a major capital ship programme, commenced pre 1914, the United States Navy was woefully weak in modern ships at the start of the European war in 1914, and the need rapidly became apparent for massive destroyer construction. Drawing on the lessons of the early years of the war, as seen in the United States, a basic destroyer design was rapidly produced that subsequently became known as the 'flush deck' or 'four stack' type. Only the first description is strictly accurate: all the ships did have flush deck lines and they introduced this hull form into American destroyer design for the first time. However, while the majority of the ships did have four stacks, some of the early ones had only three (with a thicker centre funnel to serve two boilers), and earlier USN designs had also had four stacks.

273 'Flushdeckers' were finally completed for service, and there were numerous variations on the original design. Indeed, with such a large programme contracted in a very short period (three years) variations were inevitable as shortages of components became apparent. The United States Navy therefore laid down the basic dimensions, armament, type of propulsion and contract speed. The two main contractors then developed their own concept within those parameters and Bethlehem Steel and Bath Iron Works accordingly standardised the pattern, up to DD 195. Thereafter, with the increasing pace of construction and wartime supply problems, even greater variations had to be permitted so that eventually dimensions, hull form, armament and contract speed became almost the only guide lines. With the unusual flush deck hull with its marked sheer, and four funnels in the majority, to a casual glance all ships appeared identical.

It is tempting to compare these ships with the earliest V class destroyers of the Royal Navy with which they are contemporary. Dimensions and speed are very similar, the Americans having a foot greater beam and there is an identical gun armament, but here the similarity ceases. The American hull had much finer lines than the British, fore and aft, and despite the sheer a good deal less freeboard forward. Inevitably therefore, they were wet ships, and this was compounded by the presence of a large access hatch for the forward messdecks ahead of the forward 4″ gun.

Unlike British and European practice, the USN chose to mount two of the four 4″ guns high up on the beam on top of the midships deckhouse. Not only did this restrict beam fire to three guns (unlike the British superimposed design) but it also placed a considerable weight high up on either beam somewhat negating the stability gained over the V class by the extra beam.

The torpedo armament was also unique to American practice. Their Fleet doctrine called for massed attack on a battleline, and rather than tackle the almost insuperable problem of reloading torpedoes in a small ship, the United States Navy chose to double the number of tubes so that the ships carried four triple mountings where contemporary vessels were content with two twin or triple mountings. The concept was for an attack to be delivered with a broadside of six torpedoes, followed by a 180 degree turn and a further attack. Unfortunately, in practice the projection of the beam mounted tubes over the ships' side caused the lips to dip into the slightest swell, especially when turning at other than slow speed. In consequence, a turn at attacking speed in other than a flat calm became impossible without risking damage to the mountings and/or the torpedoes. Deck space was in any case severely limited by the mountings, and the side weight caused seakeeping problems.

During service, two other problems due to hull design became evident. The fine after end cramped deck space for anti-submarine weapons (not envisaged at the time of design) and the tips of the propellers projected well beyond the ship's side aft. While this latter was quite usual in all destroyers, the extent was much greater in this design, despite the provision of heavy propeller guards aft, the incidence of damage to blades when manoeuvring alongside was high. Secondly, the connection between steering wheel and rudder head was similar to that in use in small merchantmen and trawlers, a physical chain and wire connection led along the upper deck. Inevitably wear occurred and the gear was likely to suffer weather damage and jamming due to debris, often of course at the most inopportune moment. The incidence of steering failure in the class was high, resulting in frequent collisions, despite the practice, while in British service, of renewing all the gear at intervals as short as three months.

Unlike British practice, the ship was conned and fought from an enclosed bridge which also contained the wheel and telegraphs, the upper bridge having only the most rudimentary equipment. In Royal Navy service this upper bridge was extended and re-equipped (or totally replaced) to conform to British requirements. It was also found, by bitter experience and some loss of life, that the original structure was quite incapable of withstanding severe winter weather in the North Atlantic.

The effect of North Atlantic weather on the original type of TOWN class bridge   *courtesy Ron Giles Esq.*

ACQUISITION BY GREAT BRITAIN

During April and May 1940 the British destroyer force suffered considerable depletion due to casualties and damage in the Norwegian and Low Countries fighting; depletion that new construction could not affect until early 1941. The further losses arising from the fall of France, and the need to provide the Mediterranean Fleet solely from British resources were still in the future.

On 15 May 1940, the British Ambassador in Paris advised that his American colleague there had spoken of the possibility of the French acquiring twelve older destroyers from America, apparently on the American Ambassador's initiative, and enquiry was raised if Britain would like "fifty or a hundred such ships". The response was immediate, a telegram the same day from the Prime Minister advised that the Admiralty would like 16 modern destroyers, 32 flush deckers, and 1,000 close range AA weapons. The matter rested in diplomatic hands until late July by which time the losses at Dunkirk and the (apparent) threat of imminent defeat sharpened minds on both sides of the Atlantic. By 25 July the First Sea Lord was suggesting in a minute to the First Lord that USN crews might bring the ships over to the UK, and also raising the possibility of the supply of fifty PBY flying boats, the aircraft later known to Britain as the Catalina.

On 1 August, President Roosevelt suggested via the British Ambassador in Washington that he might either (a) sell fifty ships to Canada against a legal lien on British cruisers in Canada's favour so that, if defeated, Britain would cede the ships to Canada who would donate them to the USA, or (b) transfer the ships in return for the sale of base rights by Britain to the USA. Three days later Churchill rejected (a) as impracticable and (b) as undesirable but accepted the principle of lease of base rights as a basis for further negotiation. Events then moved much more speedily, so that by 17 August the Admiralty was able to ask the Royal Australian, Royal Canadian and Royal New Zealand Navies to assist in manning possible ships. The Royal Canadian Navy agreed to take six the following day, the Royal New Zealand Navy declined on 19 August and the Royal Australian Navy on 23 August due to lack of personnel (Australia was already committed to manning destroyers of the N class and New Zealand the Armed Merchant Cruiser HMS MONOWAI). On 22 August the Ambassador in Washington advised that the transfer was imminent; it was in fact agreed on 1 September and the first crews (1,000 officers and ratings) sailed that day for Halifax.

The former American AARON WARD (DD132) and ABEL P. UPSHUR (DD193). (H.M.S.s CASTLETON and CLARE) lying at Devonport immediately after arrival from Halifax. The censor has marked the pennant numbers and background for deletion

Admiralty

As a matter of interest, official policy was that the ships were to retain their American names as an act of courtesy, and the Ambassador was so advised on 28 August; the first 16 ships transferred did in fact retain and make passage under the USN names as HMS HERNDON etc. The decision to rename them after towns common to both nations was taken in early September 1940 to ease American susceptibilities. Despite an extensive search, it is clear that the relevant Admiralty file relating to the renaming of the ships no longer exists. It is very probable that the Admiralty simply made use of an atlas index to pick town names common to both America and Britain, once the decision to use that nomenclature had been taken. The first batch of names was promulgated in early October, the balance at intervals thereafter. In view of his long personal interest in the naming of warships, it is not unlikely that the Prime Minister, Winston Churchill, may have been the person who decided on the use of town names common to both nations although there has been a suggestion that Captain Tapprell Dorling, D.S.O., Royal Navy, may have been involved.

PREPARATION AND ALTERATION FOR BRITISH SERVICE

The fifty ships chosen for transfer, some of them active, some in reserve and two actually stricken from the US Navy List, were all brought forward and commissioned by the USN, and steamed by American crews to Halifax NS. Here, after a two day introductory period where British and American personnel were onboard together and took the ships to sea for a day, the American Colours were hauled down (initially totally without ceremony, despite reports to the contrary) and the ships commissioned as HM Ships under their American names; for example HMS CHURCHILL was initially commissioned as HMS HERNDON.

An example of the corroded rivet problems, BURNHAM's Engineer Officer views the results in dry dock as the double bottoms vent their water content. Afloat, the process would be reversed with a fuel contamination problem
courtesy Ron Giles Esq

GEORGETOWN and ROXBOROUGH together in drydock shortly before transfer to Russia, probably the last time that they were photographed in Britain. This photograph shows extremely well the fine lines aft that so cramped the A/S armament of these ships, the depth charge rails have had to be sponsoned over the counter, smoke floats are stowed on top of the rails and the after throwers can be seen just aft of the superstructure. The extent to which the shafts and propellers extend beyond the line of the upper deck, and the need for the propeller guards, is also clearly visible　　　　　　　　　　　　*Tyne & Wear Museum, courtesy of Dr I L Buxton*

A close inspection of the ships was carried out at Halifax, and a detailed report made to Admiralty on the first fifteen (which composed what became known as the 1st and 2nd TOWN Flotillas, to use their initial title). The Inspecting Officer reported that, generally, the hulls and main machinery were in good condition, but that auxiliaries, piping and wiring were poor. All ships suffered from water in their fuel, leading to complete loss of power on several trials. This was thought to have been cured by pumping out, tank cleaning and careful fuelling. In fact, the problem was more severe in that the contamination arose due to loose, corroded, rivets in the shell plating, so the danger of contaminated fuel remained with the ships throughout their operational lives. The problem was not isolated at Halifax as dry docking was not carried out.

The Inspecting Officer disliked the enclosed bridge, commented adversely on the wire and chain steering, and produced a long list of recommended alterations to be put in hand at the first opportunity.

Amongst his comments were a number that are illuminating regarding the armament. He noted that the 4″ gun was a low, compact weapon compared with the British equivalent, but that the fixed ammunition was fragile and liable to part at the junction of shell and cartridge, whilst supply from the magazines (which had no flooding arrangements) was slow and expensive in manpower. The 3″ 23 calibre gun mounted in the ships, although capable of 75 degree elevation, could not in fact be operated beyond 40 degrees due to inability to handle it at a greater elevation. Additionally, the sights provided were not suitable for high elevation work. British depth charges would fit the DC rails of the ships, but no depth charge throwers were fitted, and would have to be supplied even though space aft was at a premium. The torpedoes supplied were of a poor model, known to run ten feet deeper than the settings.

In closing, the report called for the removal of all torpedo tubes, and their replacement by one triple mounting of British design on the centreline, together with a complete gun rearmament with British weapons. Removal of the mainmast, shortening of the foremast and removal of the after searchlight platform, were all required to improve stability.

The report had a wide circulation in Admiralty, being described as 'most interesting' and is annotated by Director of Operations (Home) to the effect that 'it appears that when the ships are brought up to date they will be equivalent to our S class'. While this comment may be regarded as somewhat uncomplimentary to the ships, it in fact reflects their standard vis a vis their Royal Navy contemporaries.

Of the fifty ships, forty four were manned on transfer by the Royal Navy and six by the Royal Canadian Navy. The British manned ships then made passage to Britain, as noted in the chronology and individual histories, for initial refit to rectify defects and to standardise them as far as possible with British equipment, or to British

BURWELL illustrates the Stage 1 refit except that she retains her original funnel height. The dark camouflage panel below the forward gun is typical of the early colour scheme of the class   *Admiralty*

practice. The majority of these refits were carried out at Devonport, some being more complete than others dependent upon the time that the individual ship was obliged to remain in dockyard hands. Where time permitted, the full Stage 1 refit was completed, which involved the following work:

1. removal of the mainmast and shortening the foremast
2. shortening the three after funnels by several feet
3. removing the after 4" and 3" guns, and shipping a British 12pdr HA in lieu, mounted in X position
4. removal of the two after sets of torpedo tubes
5. fitting British depth charge throwers
6. fitting ASDIC where the equivalent USN gear not already fitted, and fitting British trace recorders in all ships.

As the war progressed, and the need for longer refits became apparent, the opportunity was taken to incorporate any of the above alterations not made initially, and also to progress ships to the Stage 2 condition.

Sometimes alterations took place gradually rather than as a result of a single operation, but the final outcome was remarkably similar throughout the class, involving:

1. removing the beam 4″ guns and fitting single, manual, 20 mm Oerlikon in lieu
2. removing the remaining (forward) torpedo tubes and installing one triple British mounting on the centre line aft of the funnels
3. fitting Type 286 radar at the masthead
4. fitting Type 271 radar atop the bridge structure

This configuration was common to almost all the North Atlantic ships. Typically, 60 depth charges were carried when on anti-submarine escort duty.

Further alteration took place as additional equipment became available, thus a number of the Atlantic escorts received the ahead throwing weapon Hedgehog forward of the bridge, and HF/DF on its associated tall mast aft.

BROADWAY shows the Stage 2 refit complete with Hedgehog but without the major refit to the bridge structure. Note the Chinese-style eye painted towards the bow   *Admiralty*

Three of the class (BRADFORD, CLARE and STANLEY) were selected for even more extensive changes, probably due to their need for major refit immediately upon arrival. All three were similarly converted, and were the first ships of the Long Range Escort type, predating the conversion of the British V class ships by several months. The conversion involved the removal of the two forward boilers (and their associated funnels) and replacement by additional oil fuel tanks stowing an extra 80 tons of fuel, accommodation and stores spaces being worked in above the tanks. A new British destroyer type bridge was constructed, and the ASDIC fit updated. The reduced boiler power available gave the ships a sea speed of 25 knots, while the extra 80 tons of fuel boosted their range.

CLARE, one of three Long-Range Escort conversions on completion of her first refit   *Admiralty*

BUILDERS AND BUILDING DATA

Name	Type	Builders	Laid down	Launched	Commissioned
ANNAPOLIS	C	Union Iron Works	4.7.1918	29.9.1918	25.7.1919
BATH	C	Newport News SB Co	19.1.1918	8.6.1918	21.3.1919
BELMONT	A	Newport News SB Co	10.7.1918	21.12.1918	22.12.1919
BEVERLEY	A	Newport News SB Co	25.10.1918	19.4.1919	3.4.1920
BRADFORD	A	Bethlehem Steel, Squantum	20.4.1918	22.9.1918	5.9.1919
BRIGHTON	C	Bethlehem Steel Fore River	15.7.1918	23.11.1918	17.3.1919
BROADWATER	A	Newport News SB Co	10.7.1918	8.3.1919	28.2.1920
BROADWAY	A	Newport News SB Co	20.8.1918	14.2.1920	8.6.1920
BURNHAM	A	Bethlehem Steel Quincy	3.2.1918	11.4.1919	26.7.1919
BURWELL	A	Bethlehem Steel Squantum	20.4.1918	25.8.1918	17.3.1919
BUXTON	A	Bethlehem Steel Squantum	20.4.1918	10.10.1918	24.4.1919
CALDWELL	B	Bath Iron Works	7.10.1918	29.5.1919	12.6.1919
CAMERON	A	Bethlehem Steel Quincy	13.11.1918	8.5.1919	2.9.1919
CAMPBELTOWN	B	Bath Iron Works	29.6.1918	2.1.1919	20.1.1919
CASTLETON	B	Bath Iron Works	1.8.1918	10.4.1919	21.4.1919
CHARLESTOWN	C	Newport News SB Co	5.4.1918	4.7.1919	18.7.1919
CHELSEA	B	Bath Iron Works	5.11.1918	24.7.1919	6.8.1919
CHESTERFIELD	A	Newport News SB Co	24.9.1918	6.3.1920	25.6.1920
CHURCHILL	A	Newport News SB Co	25.11.1918	31.5.1919	17.4.1920
CLARE	A	Newport News SB Co	20.8.1918	14.2.1920	21.5.1920
COLUMBIA	C	Seattle Dry Dock	30.3.1918	4.7.1918	6.6.1919
GEORGETOWN	C	Bethlehem Steel Fore River	20.7.1918	27.10.1918	10.3.1919
HAMILTON	C	Bethlehem Steel Fore River	17.8.1918	21.12.1918	29.3.1919
LANCASTER	B	Bath Iron Works	1.9.1917	25.7.1918	25.8.1918
LEAMINGTON	B	New York SB Co	23.1.1918	28.9.1918	28.7.1919
LEEDS	D	Cramp	16.10.1916	21.8.1917	12.1.1918
LEWES	D	Norfolk Navy Yard	20.11.1917	29.6.1918	19.10.1918
LINCOLN	B	Cramp	12.2.1918	19.6.1918	29.11.1918
LUDLOW	D	Cramp	16.10.1916	17.7.1917	26.11.1917
MANSFIELD	B	Bath Iron Works	28.12.1917	30.10.1918	11.11.1918
MONTGOMERY	B	Bath Iron Works	26.6.1917	25.6.1918	31.7.1918
NEWARK	C	Union Iron Works	20.10.1917	14.4.1918	14.11.1918
NEWMARKET	C	Union Iron Works	31.10.1917	28.3.1918	19.10.1918
NEWPORT	C	Bethlehem Steel Fore River	25.8.1917	16.12.1917	14.5.1918
NIAGARA	C	Bethlehem Steel Fore River	8.6.1918	31.8.1918	14.1.1919
RAMSEY	A	Bethlehem Steel Squantum	23.9.1918	24.5.1919	8.9.1919
READING	A	Bethlehem Steel Squantum	3.6.1918	5.2.1919	27.6.1919
RICHMOND	B	Mare Island Navy Yard	10.7.1917	15.12.1917	6.4.1918
RIPLEY	A	Bethlehem Steel Squantum	3.6.1918	31.12.1918	3.7.1919
ROCKINGHAM	A	Bethlehem Steel Squantum	27.8.1918	7.5.1919	31.7.1919
ROXBOROUGH	C	Bethlehem Steel Fore River	7.8.1918	14.12.1918	21.3.1919

ST ALBANS	C	Newport News SB Co	23.3.1918	4.7.1918	25.4.1919
ST CLAIR	C	Union Iron Works	25.3.1918	4.7.1918	1.3.1919
ST CROIX	A	Bethlehem Steel Quincy	11.9.1918	31.1.1919	30.4.1919
ST FRANCIS	A	Bethlehem Steel Quincy	4.11.1918	21.3.1919	30.6.1919
ST MARYS	C	Newport News SB Co	11.5.1918	19.10.1918	26.8.1919
SALISBURY	B	Mare Island Navy Yard	25.4.1918	15.1.1919	13.9.1919
SHERWOOD	A	Bethlehem Steel Quincy	25.9.1918	26.4.1919	22.7.1919
STANLEY	A	Bethlehem Steel Quincy	25.9.1918	28.3.1919	19.5.1919
WELLS	B	Charleston Navy Yard	29.7.1918	7.7.1919	30.4.1921

	Type A	Type B	Type C	Type D
Displacement, standard	1190	1090	1060	1020
Displacement, deep	1725	1530	1530	1445
Length oa	314' 4"	314' 4"	314' 4"	315' 6"
Beam, maximum	31' 8"	31'	31' 8"	31' 2"
Mean draught, deep	12' 10"	11' 11"	11' 11"	11'
Machinery	geared turbines	geared turbines	geared turbines	direct drive turbines (LEWES geared)
Shafts	2	2	2	3 (LEWES 2)
Speed, deep in 1941	28.5 kts	28.75 kts	29.75 kts	30 kts
Boilers	4	4	4	4
Armament 1940	4×1 4"	4×1 4"	4×1 4"	4×1 3"/50 cal
	1×1 3"/23 cal	1×1 3"/23 cal	1×1 3"/23 cal	1×1 3"/23 cal
	4×3 21"TT	4×3 21"TT	4×3 21"TT	4×3 21"TT

OIL FUEL

In the usual statistics of a ship, oil fuel stowage is a meaningless term unless related to a speed, consumption, and therefore a radius of action. In the TOWN class destroyers, those with USN hull numbers up to and including DD 185 stowed 275 tons (British records show between 268 tons and 284 tons for these ships). At a speed of 10 knots, this equated to an endurance of just over 2,000 miles. DD 186 onwards stowed 375 tons (by American records) or 390 tons (by British records) which gave them an endurance of just over 2,900 miles at 10 knots.

The Long Range Escort conversions stowed an additional 80 tons to give approximately 3,500 miles endurance.

While a normal convoy speed was 9 knots or less, allowance must be made for the extra speed employed by escorts, and the need to keep steam at all occasions. The official Admiralty tables specifically state that "Allowance should be made for additional steaming while on convoy duty. War experience indicates that this distance increase can amount to 33%." In effect, therefore, the endurance of even a long legged LRE escort could be reduced to 2,300 miles, while the usual North Atlantic convoy in 1941 logged 2,000 miles, on passage. It must also be borne in mind that the figures quoted are for ships six months out of dock with steam for full speed at 30 minutes notice.

Individual performances showed considerable variations, LEWES for some reason apparently requiring 1.9 tons per hour at ten knots against the normal 1.25 tons per hour; perhaps a reflection on her antique power plant.

All in all, it behoves any reader to take quoted range, radius, or endurance figures in any publication with reservation.

SERVICE AFTER TRANSFER

Of the 50 ships, the six manned initially by the Royal Canadian Navy remained in Canadian waters for service as local escorts. The 44 British manned ships were, as previously noted, destined for passage to Britain and brief refit prior to active service in UK waters. In fact, as the individual narratives show, certain passages were delayed due to accidents and breakdown, there was a further transfer of one ship to the Royal Canadian Navy, and later some passage of Canadian ships to Britain and refit on this side of the Atlantic.

The British manned ships, after refits of varying length and complexity, fell initially into three categories; those allocated to Rosyth for East Coast escort duty, those to the 1st Minelaying Squadron as A/S escort for the Northern Mine Barrage scheme, and finally those ships allocated for North Atlantic escort work.

In the main, the Rosyth ships remained on that duty throughout the war, while the Minelaying Squadron ships passed either to Rosyth or directly to Reserve when the Squadron disbanded in 1943. The North Atlantic ships, based initially in Britain, gradually dispersed as age took its toll of them, passing either to local duty in Canadian waters, to second line duty such as Air Target Ships (ATS), or to Reserve. Few proceeded beyond the UK/Halifax, NS area of operations, although the 'long legged' CLARE operated to Freetown, and CHURCHILL in the West Indies at one time.

HMS LEWES was the exception to all rules; when she passed to second line duty as a target vessel she was allocated to South Atlantic Command based at Capetown where she remained until 1944. Transferred then to the Eastern Fleet, based on Trincomalee, this was still not the end to her wanderings for, in 1945, she again moved her base, this time to the British Pacific Fleet based on Sydney NSW. Here she served out her days, finally being paid off, stripped of equipment, and scuttled off Sydney.

CAMPBELTOWN lying alongside BROKE at a Western Approaches base. The interest in this photograph lies in the positive evidence of this ship's manning by the Royal Netherlands Navy. It also illustrates well the features that the Censor wanted deleting: the skyline and equipment details on the left, the masthead "fits" and the pennant numbers on CAMPBELTOWN'S stern. The rating on the port propeller guard appears to wish to be "alone"   Admiralty

TOWNs seem to have been regarded as particularly dispensable ships, for example CAMPBELTOWN was manned at various times by a part Polish, a Dutch and finally a British crew. Other ships were Norwegian manned, lent to Russia etc; all these movements and loans will be found detailed in the individual histories that follow.

As the individual narratives show, the class as a whole did not become effectively operational until early 1941, well after the emergency that prompted their acquisition had passed. Unlike their British contemporaries, they also passed quite quickly from the operational scene, few of the ships serving as other than second line duty units after the end of 1943.

While there is no doubt that the TOWNs did contribute to the Royal Navy's efforts, the oft repeated quote 'fifty ships that saved the world', while emotive, is very far from fact. The act of transfer, and the situation brought about by the acquisition of sovereign rights in a belligerent's territory, certainly affected the strategic position and brought American participation in the war against the Axis nearer. The tactical effect of the ships themselves was, however, small as a study of the individual histories will demonstrate.

CHRONOLOGY

3. 9.1940	Agreement to transfer signed, and announced
7. 9.1940	1st Flotilla (8 ships) arrived in Halifax Nova Scotia (NS)
9. 9.1940	First eight ships commissioned as HMS with original USN names
10. 9.1940	Decision to rename as TOWNs taken
17. 9.1940	First eight TOWN names announced
23. 9.1940	2nd Flotilla (7 ships) commissioned, still with original USN names
24. 9.1940	Five ships taken over by Royal Canadian Navy
26. 9.1940	First five ships arrived in the UK
2.10.1940	First eight ships received TOWN names
	Sixth RCN ship and three ships of 3rd Flotilla commissioned
4.10.1940	Second eight ships received TOWN names
8.10.1940	Further seven ships commissioned with TOWN names
	Five ships arrived in the UK
23.10.1940	Further nine ships commissioned with TOWN name
24.10.1940	Four ships arrived in the UK
26.10.1940	Three ships arrived in the UK
7.11.1940	Two ships arrived in the UK
9.11.1940	Three ships arrived in the UK
10.11.1940	Three ships arrived in the UK
11.11.1940	One ship arrived in the UK
26.11.1940	Four ships commissioned
28.11.1940	Four ships arrived in the UK
5.12.1940	First loss, HMS CAMERON
	Bombed and Constructive Total Loss at Portsmouth
	Final six ships commissioned
11.12.1940	Two ships arrived in the UK
14.12.1940	Two ships arrived in the UK
19.12.1940	One ship arrived in the UK
20.12.1940	Two ships arrived in the UK
22.12.1940	Two ships arrived in the UK
30.12.1940	One ship arrived in the UK
7. 1.1941	Decision taken to man two ships with Norwegian crews
26. 1.1941	Four ships arrived in the UK
	Forty four now in the UK waters
5. 3.1941	Two ships arrived in the UK
19. 8.1941	HMS BATH (Norwegian manned) sunk, first loss at sea
11.11.1941	Last ship to transit to UK, HMS BUXTON, arrived in UK

DATES COMMISSIONED AT HALIFAX

9 September 1940 CALDWELL, CAMERON, CAMPBELTOWN, CASTLETON, CHESTERFIELD, CHELSEA, CHURCHILL, CLARE.

23 September 1940 BRIGHTON, CHARLESTOWN, GEORGETOWN, HAMILTON, ROXBOROUGH, ST ALBANS, ST MARYS.

24 September 1940 COLUMBIA, NIAGARA, ST CLAIR, ST CROIX, ST FRANCIS.

2 October 1940 ANNAPOLIS, BATH, BROADWATER, LUDLOW.

8 October 1940 BELMONT, BEVERLEY, BRADFORD, BROADWAY, BURNHAM, BUXTON, BURWELL.

23 October 1940 LANCASTER, LEAMINGTON, LEEDS, LEWES, LINCOLN, MANSFIELD, MONTGOMERY, SHERWOOD, STANLEY.

26 November 1940 RAMSEY, READING, RIPLEY, ROCKINGHAM, plus NEWARK, NEWMARKET, NEWPORT, RICHMOND, WELLS to Care and Maintenance.

5 December 1940 NEWARK, NEWMARKET, NEWPORT, RICHMOND, SALISBURY, WELLS.

PENNANT LIST — DECODE

G 05	LANCASTER	I 05	CAMERON
G 08	NEWARK	I 07	ROXBOROUGH
G 19	LEAMINGTON	I 08	BRIGHTON
G 27	LEEDS	I 12	ST MARYS
G 42	LINCOLN	I 14	CLARE
G 47	NEWMARKET	I 15	ST ALBANS
G 54	NEWPORT	I 17	BATH
G 57	LUDLOW	I 20	CALDWELL
G 58	ROCKINGHAM	I 21	CHARLESTOWN
G 60	RAMSEY	I 23	CASTLETON
G 68	LEWES	I 24	HAMILTON
G 71	READING	I 28	CHESTERFIELD
G 76	MANSFIELD	I 35	CHELSEA
G 79	RIPLEY	I 40	GEORGETOWN
G 88	RICHMOND	I 42	CAMPBELTOWN
G 95	MONTGOMERY	I 45	CHURCHILL
H 46	BELMONT	I 49	COLUMBIA
H 64	BEVERLEY	I 52	SALISBURY
H 72	BRADFORD	I 57	NIAGARA
H 81	BROADWATER	I 65	ST CLAIR
H 82	BURNHAM	I 73	STANLEY
H 90	BROADWAY	I 80	SHERWOOD
H 94	BURWELL	I 81	ST CROIX
H 96	BUXTON	I 93	ST FRANCIS
I 04	ANNAPOLIS	I 95	WELLS

ESCORT FORCES ORGANISATION

At the time that the TOWN class entered British service, the organisation of escort craft into Groups was a purely administrative matter. Groups were numbered consecutively from 1st Escort Group, the system being limited to escort vessels operating from UK bases. So far as possible, the escort for a convoy would be drawn from the same Group; however quite frequently in 1941 an outward convoy escort would have to be formed from what was available rather than desirable.

With the advent of American escorts in the Western Atlantic, signal traffic made much more use of the USN Task Unit designation system; however Commander in Chief Western Approaches, and the Royal Canadian Navy, designated certain Groups to work the North Atlantic convoy system, and numbered these A (American) B (British) and C (Canadian) followed by a numeric commencing at 1 for each alpha series. Those British Groups not dedicated specifically to the trans Atlantic convoy route, retained plain numeric designations eg 2nd Escort Group. There were certain gaps in the numeration of British Groups, but the pattern was that those in the series 40th EG onward were employed on the West African convoy route, while the lower figure Groups handled the Gibraltar traffic, or acted as Support Groups.

With the withdrawal of American forces from the main North Atlantic escort duty in 1943, the A Group designation lapsed, thereafter all convoys were escorted by B or C Groups, Groups with plain numeration eg 2 EG acted in the main in the Support role, while the higher figures eg 40 EG remained on the Freetown/UK route. Groups were designated 2nd; 12th etc, but for brevity were frequently referred to as '2EG', a style which is used in this text as an alternate form. Certain general terms were also used in referring to escorts, which also need explanation, especially in relation to the TOWNS, these are set out below

1st Minelaying Squadron	The converted merchantmen based at Kyle of Lochalsh to lay and maintain the Northern Barrage. A number of TOWNS were attached for escort duty, and were also employed as a "pool" from which escorts could be drawn for important convoys (usually the WS series), Icelandic ferry convoys, and other special duties.
Rosyth Escort Force	The ships based on Rosyth responsible for the northern end of the East Coast convoy series FS and FN.
Newfoundland Escort Force (NEF)	Formed in mid 1941, based on St Johns NF, and responsible for North Atlantic convoys between St Johns meeting point and a mid ocean meeting point off Iceland.
Mid Ocean Escort Force (MOEF)	A Royal Canadian Navy title, applied to those Groups dedicated to the St Johns NF to Londonderry part of the trans Atlantic convoy route. The successor organisation to the Newfoundland Escort Force.
Western Local Escort Force (WLEF)	Local only in the sense that it operated in Canadian home waters. Based on Halifax NS the WLEF was responsible for the escort of convoys between New York City, Halifax and onward to St Johns NF meeting point where the MOEF took over, a passage of some 600 miles.
Western Escort Force (WEF)	The later variant title applied to WLEF
Western Support Force (WSF)	Formed in 1943 to operate in support of endangered convoys. A short lived organisation due to the poor maintenance record of the ships allocated.
A Groups	American commanded Groups dedicated to North Atlantic convoy escort, generally contained a major proportion of Canadian ships.
B Groups	British Groups, occasionally containing Allied ships, dedicated to North Atlantic convoy escort.
C Groups	Canadian Groups, sometimes with a British Senior Officer ship in 1942 and 1943, dedicated to North Atlantic convoy escort.
Support Group	An Escort Group, usually numeric eg 2 EG but occasionally a B Group specially deployed, which was employed in the support role, ie not specifically allocated to convoy and not charged with the escort of convoy as its prime duty, thus able to remain with a contact or transfer to another, more threatened, convoy.
Air Target Ships (ATS)	Ships, usually old destroyers, employed as torpedo targets for training carrier borne aircraft. The requirement was for a fast, agile ship surplus to operational needs, and not equipped for the escort role, thus reducing complement at a time of acute man-power shortage. Hence the ships, usually, landed all A/S equipment (including radar) torpedo tubes, HF/DF etc.

GLOSSARY OF TERMS AND DESCRIPTIONS

AA	Anti aircraft.
A/S	Anti Submarine.
ASDIC	A submarine detection apparatus, now known as SONAR.
DC	Depth Charge. A drumshaped container holding 300lb of explosive actuated by a hydrostatic fuze housed in a tube running the length of the axis of the charge. As the war progressed, new explosives (MINOL and later TORPEX) greatly increased the explosive power for the same weight.
DC (Heavy)	A standard charge but with additional ballast strapped to it to increase its rate of sinking.
DC (Light)	The standard depth charge.
DCT	Depth Charge Thrower, usually referred to as 'throwers'. A mortar, originally with a separate carrying tray, used to project depth charges some distance from the firing ship to its beam. Later versions had the carrier integral to the thrower, saving material, time and effort.
HA	High Angle ie anti aircraft capable.
HF/DF	High Frequency Direction Finding. A receiving apparatus which automatically received High Frequency transmissions, and indicated their bearing accurate to one degree, from a very brief signal. Therefore invaluable in indicating the presence of a German submarine, which used HF extensively to communicate with home bases. Usually referred to as 'HuffDuff' in the period 1939/45.
Hedgehog	The first Ahead Throwing Weapon, projecting 24 contact fuzed bombs from a spigot mortar mounting on an escort's focsle. Thus the attacking ship retained ASDIC contact up to the moment of firing, and the target had no warning. Introduced in 1942.
Mk X	A heavy depth charge containing 2,000 lb of explosive in a case 21" in diameter. Carried in, and projected from, a destroyer's torpedo tubes. Used to 'stir up' submarines lying silent and deep; it was fuzed from 500' to 900'.
LA	Low angle ie surface weapons.
RDF	Radio Direction Finding now known as RADAR. Sets carried a three figure type designator, the commonest in escort use being:
RDF 286	A masthead aerial, originally fixed, later rotating, used to detect approaching aircraft. Introduced in early 1941, initially crude and of little use for anti submarine work.
RDF 271	A rotating 'cheese' aerial contained within a distinctive 'lantern housing'. Centimetric, recording its trace on a Plan Position Indicator (PPI) screen. Very effective even in its initial form, and much developed during the war after its initial introduction in mid 1941. Of immense value to escorts, both for creating a 'radar fence' against surfaced submarines, and for station keeping and general search.
RDF 291	A masthead aerial of St Andrews Cross form, used for air warning and superseding type 286.
SW1C	Surface Warning 1st Canadian. The first Canadian produced radar, equivalent to the British 286. Theoretically good, in service a very poor performer; it also suffered from being developed at the time that 286 was phased out and replaced by 271, a vast step in radar technology that the Canadian set could not match.
Rails	Horizontal track stowing depth charges and projecting over the transom of an escort, enabling charges to be released at a set rate. In conjunction with the throwers, enabled a pattern of charges to be laid over a target.
Trace recorders	An electro mechanical device which recorded on sensitized paper the transmissions and return echoes of ASDIC. The presence of a target could thus be more readily identified. together with its range, depth and bearing. By the use of mathematically designed cursors the depth charge firing position could be predicted, and transmitted automatically to the firing positions. Developed pre 1939 by the Royal Navy, vastly increased the effectiveness of depth charge patterns, and supplied to the USN for its use in 1941.

SHIPS' HISTORIES

Photographed late in her career, ANNAPOLIS still has SW1C radar at the foremast but has shipped the far more effective 271 radar atop her rebuilt, British style, bridge. The ahead throwing Hedgehog is on the starboard side forward of the bridge, she has single 20 mm in the beam 4" gun positions, and the shield of the British 12pdr HA can be seen aft. The absence of beam torpedo tubes indicates that she has shipped a centreline mounting. Note the absence of the fourth funnel, this and its associated boiler were removed after the boiler burnt out due to mishandling shortly after transfer; it is possible that the space was utilised to extend the oil fuel capacity
courtesy K. Macpherson

HMCS ANNAPOLIS I 04 (ex USS MACKENZIE, DD 175)

ANNAPOLIS commissioned in the Royal Canadian Navy at Halifax 29.9.40, and almost immediately suffered severe boiler damage due to inexperienced personnel, No. 4 boiler being burnt out. Under repair at the hard pressed Halifax Dockyard until 2.41, the damaged unit was removed together with its funnel; thereafter ANNAPOLIS was employed exclusively in Canadian waters.

With the arrival of newly built escorts in quantity, ANNAPOLIS paid off to become a static training ship attached to HMCS CORNWALLIS, the Halifax shore establishment, on 8.4.44, remaining on that service until 4.6.45. Sold for scrap to Frankel Bros on 21.6.45, she was towed away to Boston the following day.

Photographed very early in her Royal Navy career, BATH shows only RN camouflage and pennants (obliterated by the censor) and the loss of her after torpedo tubes. The after 4" and 3" guns are still mounted, neither have her funnels been cut down
courtesy K. Macpherson

HMS BATH I 17 (ex USS HOPEWELL, DD 181)

Commissioned on 23.9.40 at Halifax, BATH sailed on 29.9 for Devonport via St John's NF and Belfast, arriving 12.10 for a brief refit before joining the 1st Minelaying Squadron based in HMS TRELAWNEY at Port ZA, in fact the Kyle of Lochalsh. She escorted four minelaying sorties by the Squadron, and provided local A/S escort for three major troop convoys (WS4B, WS5A and TC8) after which she went to Chatham for refit from 25.1 to 12.4.41.

During the Chatham refit, the standard Stage 1 alterations were made, and on completion she was manned by Royal Norwegian Navy personnel, transfer actually taking place 9.4.41. Unfortunately her return to active duty was delayed by a collision when on trials on 16.4 and the ship repaired on the Tyne until 19.5, followed by a work up at Tobermory until 18.6.41.

On completion of work up, BATH joined 5th Escort Group based at Liverpool and was principally engaged in escorting the OG/HG convoys to and from Gibraltar. While escorting her sixth convoy, OG71, she was torpedoed by U204 on 19.8.41 in 48.30N 17.45W, and sank rapidly.

HMS BELMONT H 46 (ex USS SATTERLEE, DD 190)

BELMONT commissioned at Halifax 8.10.40, and sailed for Devonport and refit 15.10, arriving 28.10. Refit was completed 25.11, but trials and defects delayed the ship at Devonport and Milford Haven so that she did not arrive at Scapa Flow for work up until 5.1.41. Further defects and a collision off the Isle of Man 22.3.41 put her into the repairer's hands at Liverpool after escorting only one convoy and she did not become fully operational with 3rd Escort Group until 20.8.41, ten and a half months after transfer at Halifax.

BELMONT remained based at Liverpool, escorting convoys in the Western Approaches, until 30.11.41 when she sailed for St. John's NF to take up local escort duty there. Service in Canadian waters was brief for, while escorting her third convoy from St John's (troop convoy NA2) she was torpedoed by U81 on 31.1.42 in 42.02N 57.18W, and sank with the loss of her entire ship's company.

Almost stopped in a calm sea, BELMONT was presumably photographed late in 1941 prior to her transfer to Canadian waters. She shows the usual Stage 1 alterations, but has acquired 286 radar at the masthead, indicating the dating. The prominent propeller guards show up well in this picture
National Maritime Museum

A poor aerial shot of BEVERLEY, but one of the rarer illustrations of the ship from a Canadian source. Particularly it shows the cramped state of the quarter deck with barely room for the two after depth charge throwers and two short sets of DC rails
courtesy K. Macpherson

While not the best of photographs, this does show BEVERLEY in Stage 2 configuration with wing position 20 mm, 271 radar atop a rebuilt bridge, centreline torpedo tubes, a 12 pdr HA aft and Hedgehog forward of the bridge
Admiralty

HMS BEVERLEY H 64 (ex USS BRANCH, DD 197)

BEVERLEY transferred at Halifax 8.10.40 and arrived at Devonport for initial refit on 25.10. Completing trials 19.11, she carried out local escort work until allocated to 6th Escort Group of Western Approaches Command, with which she escorted convoys outward from the UK north of Ireland, to return with inward bound ships. During this period, engine defects necessitated a major refit on the Tyne from 3.41 to 31.5.41

Briefly joining Iceland Command on completion of refit, BEVERLEY then transferred to the UK/Gibraltar route escorting 9th Motor Launch Flotilla to Gibraltar and returning with an HG convoy prior to a further six weeks in dockyard hands, this time at Belfast, during 8 and 9.41, during which 286 radar was fitted.

After working up post refit, BEVERLEY rejoined 6th EG and operated in the North Atlantic escorting trade convoys and five major troop convoys before transferring to B1 Group early in 1942.

While serving with B1, BEVERLEY formed part of the escort for two Russian convoys, PQ14 and QP11, the latter having several brushes with German surface forces in very poor weather. Following these two convoys, the ship went to the repairers at Belfast and from mid 5 to 8.42 her equipment was upgraded by the addition of 271 radar mounted on a new bridge, Hedgehog, centreline torpedo tubes plus the supply of the one ton Mk X depth charges for them. On completion of this refit, the ship transferred to B4 Group.

With B4, BEVERLEY formed part of the initial escort for the troop convoy WS22, returning from that as part of the escort for HMS RAMILLIES: thereafter she was engaged exclusively in the North Atlantic war. During this period, while escorting SC118 she was in a minor collision with *ADAMAS* fortunately escaping major damage.

BEVERLEY was one of the escorts for convoy HX229 in 3.43, the high point of the convoy war following which there was a dramatic change in Allied fortunes at sea in the Atlantic.

On 9.4.43, while part of the escort of convoy ON176. BEVERLEY collided with the *CAIRNVALONA*, the damage including the loss of her Asdic capability. She was, therefore, unaware of the presence of U188 on 11.4, and was torpedoed and sunk with the loss of all but four of the ship's company of 152.

Unfortunately a poor photograph, but the only known illustration of BRADFORD, thought to have been taken by a Canadian rating at Londonderry. It shows the ship after her conversion to a Long Range Escort, and must be dated between 10.41 and 10.42, as she has 271 radar (just visible) but no Hedgehog, these two items being fitted in 10.41 and 10.42 respectively
courtesy K. Macpherson

HMS BRADFORD H 72 (ex USS McLANAHAN, DD 264)

Commissioned on 8.10.40, and briefly refitted at Devonport between 29.10 and 12.11, BRADFORD was selected for conversion in consequence of defects arising during her work up period. The refit, of considerable extent, was undertaken at Sheerness and, together with trials, associated defects and a collision, meant that she did not become operational with 43rd Escort Group on the UK/ Gibraltar convoy route until 10.41, one year after transfer.

It is apparent that, despite the long refit, all was not well with BRADFORD as she returned to a repair yard on Humberside from 6 to 8.42. Even after that, she escorted only three convoys (one in the North Atlantic, KMS2 to Operation TORCH, and a return convoy from that invasion of North Africa), during which she was in collision and went aground. In mid 12.42 therefore BRADFORD again went into dockyard hands, this time at Liverpool. By mid 1943 it had become apparent that the ship was beyond economic repair, and she paid off into the control of Devonport Command, being towed away from Liverpool on 14.5.43. On arrival at Devonport, she was commissioned on 1.6.43 as HMS FFOLIOTT, an accommodation ship and accounting base for Combined Operations personnel, and she served as such for the rest of the war. She was handed over for scrapping on 19.6.46, and arrived in tow at Troon in 8.46 for work to commence by the West of Scotland Shipbreaking Co. Ltd.

BRIGHTON, shown here in Stage 1 refit state, with beam 4" still mounted and the beam torpedo tubes forward. The bridge is still unaltered. Photographed in late 1940 Admiralty

BRIGHTON is shown above, almost certainly, at Tail of the Bank during her post refit trials. Her bridge has been somewhat extended with 271 radar fitted, the wing 4" guns replaced by 20 mm and a triple centreline torpedo tube mounting replaces the beam mounting. The newly completed cruiser SCYLLA lies at anchor beyond BRIGHTON Imperial War Museum

HMS BRIGHTON I 08 (ex USS COWELL, DD 167)

Commissioned at Halifax 23.9.40, BRIGHTON arrived at Devonport 12.10 for refit. She eventually completed and sailed 17.1.41, to join the 1st Minelaying Squadron at Kyle of Lochalsh as an A/S escort. Here, she escorted the first of the Icelandic military ferry convoys (DS1/SD1), the initial stage of troop convoy WS8X, and several minelaying sorties. During one such on 25.6.41 she was in collision with the cruiser KENYA and was towed to Iceland for temporary repair. Towed from Iceland to the Clyde, she arrived 2.7 and remained in the yard until 25.9; further defects developed during trials so that it was not until 16.10 that her new crew took her to Tobermory to work up until 26.10.

Returning to the 1st Minelaying Squadron, BRIGHTON escorted two further lays and another Icelandic convoy cycle before needing further repairs on the Clyde from 8.12 to 30.3.42, including Stage 2 alterations.

Taken at the same time as the lower photograph on the facing page, this view of BRIGHTON shows the bridge structure clearly and also the 291 radar at the masthead. Radar and pennant number have been marked by the censor for deletion
Admiralty

In 11.42, with the Minelaying Squadron due to be disbanded and BRIGHTON in need of further repair, it was decided to reduce the ship to second line duty as an Air Target Ship for the Fleet Air Arm. In addition to a general refit, this involved the removal of much of the A/S armament to reduce complement and lighten the ship, and the fitting of deck stowage and gear for the recovery of practice torpedoes. Completed for this service in 5.43, BRIGHTON was employed initially in the Irish Sea and Clyde Approaches until 1.44. From that date, she moved to the East Coast of Scotland, and celebrated her arrival by a collision with the trawler *STAR OF THE WAVE,* on 13.1.44, thereafter repairing at Invergordon. Surveyed during this work, it was decided not to proceed further with repairs and the ship was placed in Reserve on the Tyne in early 3.44.

During 1944 the question arose of the disposal of the Italian Fleet, the intention being that the victors should share the spoils. With the war still in progress, and Italy now an ally, the question and possible solutions were politically undesirable. Nevertheless, Russia persisted in her demand for immediate delivery of her share, a claim which was difficult to meet given the political and strategic problems in 1944. In order to calm the situation, comparable replacement tonnage was arranged, a British battleship, an American cruiser and nine British destroyers being transferred on loan to Russia pending a post war distribution of the Italian ships.

The destroyers chosen for transfer to the Russian Northern Fleet (the only area to which delivery was possible in 1944) were the TOWN ships laid up in reserve in the UK. BRIGHTON was one of these, and she accordingly refitted on the Tyne in 5.44, transferring to Russia as ZHARKI on 16.7.44. In company with her sisters, she sailed to her new base at Kola Inlet during the passage of convoy JW59, arriving on 25.8.44.

Details of her Russian service are scant, but were probably restricted to local operations out of Kola and Murmansk. BRIGHTON was returned to the Royal Navy at Rosyth on 4.3.49. Not surprisingly she was adjudged worn out and of no further use, and she was passed to the breakers 5.4, arriving at Bo'ness on 18.5.49 to be scrapped by P. & W. MacLellan Ltd.

With a background that appears Irish rather than Newfoundland, and with 286 radar indicating mid 6.41, it seems that this photograph was taken just prior to BROADWATER departing on 28.6 to join the Newfoundland Escort Force. A typical Stage 1 conversion, the first and fourth funnels are there, their camouflage pattern just merges them into the background   *courtesy K. Macpherson*

HMS BROADWATER H 81 (ex USS MASON, DD 191)

Commissioned at Halifax, refit work was carried out at Devonport, and later Cardiff, completing 31.1.41. Allocated initially to 11th Escort Group, BROADWATER's first duty was as escort to convoy WS6, during which she contracted boiler defects that forced her to return to the Clyde for two weeks repair. She then escorted the next WS convoy (WS7) and later HG56 and OB306. BROADWATER seems to have been one of the class dogged by defects, for further work was then required on the Clyde from 9 to 17.4, followed by a long refit which started at Southampton and lasted to 9.6 and completed at Portsmouth 20.6.41.

After all this work, BROADWATER sailed with convoy OB339 on 28.6, en route to join the Newfoundland Escort Force covering the St John's NF to Iceland convoy passage, and she continued on this route until 19.10.41 when, with convoy SC48, she was torpedoed by U101 and sunk in 57.01N 19.08W.

Possibly taken on the same occasion as the following illustration, the Hedgehog mounting forward on BROADWAY shows very clearly here. Taken in approximately 3.42   *Admiralty*

A nice view from the quarter of BROADWAY shows the usual Stage 2 alterations. Note that while 20 mm Oerlikons are mounted abeam the funnels, the two bandstands aft are still occupied by what appear to be .5" machine guns
Admiralty

HMS BROADWAY H 90 (ex USS HUNT, DD 194)

BROADWAY commissioned at Halifax NS 8.10.40 and arrived at Devonport for refit on 20.10. The refit was completed 19.11 and she went to Scapa Flow to work up, being allocated to 11th Escort Group; however a collision at Scapa Flow on 7.12 put her into repair at Hull until 7.1.41. A further work up followed revealing yet more defects that required attention on the Clyde (2 weeks), at Liverpool (4 weeks) and finally Devonport (4 weeks). A final work up at Tobermory cleared her for service on 28.4.41, at which time she passed to 3rd Escort Group based in Iceland.

3 EG's task was to escort convoys on the mid section of the Atlantic passage and it was only eight days after the start of this work that BROADWAY became involved in one of the most important naval events of the war. As part of the escort to convoy OB318, she took part in the apparent sinking of U110, closing the surfaced submarine and in fact being herself seriously damaged when a hydroplane pierced the engineroom, an error that arose as a result of her own gunfire having shattered the pilot house windows obscuring the Commanding Officer's view of the target during his run in.

In fact, U110 did not sink although abandoned by its crew, and HMS BULLDOG (Senior Officer of the Group) got a boarding party onboard and took the submarine in tow. Part of the haul was the immediate removal of the complete machine cyphering equipment, the first occasion on which this naval version became available to Britain. The immediate effect was to allow the reading of German submarine signals at will while the settings remained unaltered and the knowledge gained from study of the equipment also permitted similar access throughout most of the rest of the war. Most important of all, the fact that the submarine sank in tow thirty six hours later, that its crew remained unaware of the boarding and capture, and that all British personnel concerned remained totally silent on the subject, kept all knowledge of the coup from the enemy.

The damage inflicted by the collision kept BROADWAY under repair for two months at Dundee, and she was transferred to 17th Escort Group based on Newfoundland on completion. After service based on St John's BROADWAY returned to Sheerness for refit in 12.41, during which she received 271 radar and Hedgehog in a refit lasting to 4.42. Following this, the ship returned to the North Atlantic and 17th EG, interspersed with a month's refit at Boston in 7.42, and at Liverpool in 9.42, when HF/DF was fitted.

Work with 17th EG continued until 12.42 when the ship was taken in hand at Belfast for refit. On completion, and after work up at Tobermory, BROADWAY became part of the Canadian C2 Group in 2.43 and escorted two convoys with them to and from North Africa (KMS11 and MKS12). These two convoys having proved the Group's efficiency, it returned to the North Atlantic scene and during its second passage BROADWAY located and sank U89 on 14.5.43.

An interesting photograph taken in April 1944 after BROADWAY became an Air Target Ship. She has been fully converted to Stage 2 complete with a new bridge and the usual adjustment of armament. Undoubtedly 271 radar was also fitted, Hedgehog, centreline tubes and HF/DF. In the target ship role all these refinements have been removed, plus the depth charge equipment aft, leaving a clear upper deck for the retrieval and stowage of torpedoes. Note that two heavy davits have been fitted amidships for recovery, the HF/DF mast remains but the aerial has been removed
Admiralty

Two further convoy escorts were completed before it became apparent that the old ship was no longer worth maintaining as an ocean escort, especially with new construction coming into service on a large scale; accordingly she refitted at Belfast as an Air Target Ship, on completion being allocated to the East coast of Scotland.

Unlike most of her sisters BROADWAY was still operating in the target role in 5.45, and had her moments of glory when she took part in the liberation of Tromso on 16.5.45. Paid off 9.8.45, BROADWAY lay in unmaintained reserve until 17.2.47 when she was allocated for scrapping, finally arriving at Charlestown in 3.48 to be broken up by Metal Industries Ltd.

From the presence of 271 radar on a newly extended bridge, but the absence of HF/DF aft, this photograph of BURNHAM was taken between 5 and 10.42. 286 radar tops the foremast, centreline tubes are fitted and, unusually, the searchlight has been replaced in its tower by a third 20 mm to augment the beam guns. The sided pennant number aft is also unusual in R.N. practice, possibly applied during her Charleston SC refit in 3.42
Admiralty

HMS BURNHAM in pre war days as USS AULICK, a good illustration of the original appearance of the type generally.

HMS BURNHAM H 82 (ex USS AULICK, DD 258)

Commissioned at Halifax 8.10.40, BURNHAM sailed for Devonport 16.10 and completed a brief refit to work up at Scapa Flow 12.11. Her first task on joining W Approaches Command was to escort the new carrier FORMIDABLE from Belfast to the Clyde, followed by bringing in convoy SL56. Weather damage incurred during this last task placed the ship under repair at Belfast from 17.12 to 30.1.1941.

Once repairs were complete, BURNHAM joined 12th Escort Group operating in UK waters; however a collision with MALCOLM on 3.3 sent her into Liverpool for repairs lasting until 27.4. On completion, the ship proceeded westward, first to Iceland where 12EG was now based, then to St John's NF in late 5.41 to join the Newfoundland Escort Force.

A further collision, this time with sister CHESTERFIELD, put BURNHAM into Boston for repair from mid 9.41 to 23.10.41, after which she resumed escort duty from St John's. In mid 3.42 the ship went South to Charleston SC for a six week refit, followed by a month's duty based on Bermuda, after which BURNHAM returned to the RCN remaining in Canadian waters until called home for refit on the Thames during 11 and 12.42.

On completion of refit and work up, BURNHAM joined the Canadian C3 Escort Group and remained on trans Atlantic escort duty until late 10.43.

By that date, the flow of new ships led to the retirement of many of the oldest escorts, so BURNHAM returned to Western Approaches Command and a refit at Liverpool for use as an Air Target Ship, lasting until 3.44.

Duty as a target lasted eight months, with BURNHAM paying off to Reserve at Milford Haven 1.12.44 where she lay until listed for disposal in 3.47 finally arriving at Pembroke Dock 2.12.48 to be broken up by R. S. Hayes.

In this photograph BURWELL still mounts the beam 4" guns, the sided torpedo tubes and 286 radar at the foremasthead; all indicate a date between 4.41 and 5.42. 20 mm have been added; they can be seen (canvas shrouded) between the first and second funnels　　　　　　　　　　　　　　　　　　　　　　　　　　*Admiralty*

HMS BURWELL H 94 (ex USS LAUB, DD 263)

Taken over at Halifax 8.10.40, BURWELL arrived at Devonport 5.11 and carried out a protracted refit completing 24.2.41. She then joined 12th Escort Group and escorted her first convoy 23.3.

In common with the rest of 12EG, BURWELL transferred during 5.41 to Iceland where she was based until moving west to St John's NF in 7.41 when the Newfoundland Escort Force was formed.

In 8.41 BURWELL was one of the ships involved in the recovery of U570 after its surrender to an aircraft of the RAF. After this excitement, the monotony of routine convoy escort was resumed until 11.41 when a refit was carried out at Boston from 14.11.41 to 3.2.42. Three further Atlantic convoys followed, then further repair was needed initially at Londonderry and then at Liverpool. The old ship must have been in a poor state, as these repairs spanned 4.42 to 1.43, followed by workup at Tobermory during 2.43.

On completion of work up, BURWELL escorted a convoy to Gibraltar and returned with a single merchantman, via the Azores. Either the ship's efficiency was low or there was an unusually early crew change, as a further work up at Tobermory followed at the end of 4.43.

BURWELL then returned to North Atlantic work with a sailing in mid 5.43, and she continued on this route until 10.43.

In 10.43, BURWELL reduced to second line duty as an Air Target Ship based in the Clyde, and served as a target for Fleet Air Arm aircraft until 1.45, arriving on 14.1.45 to lay up in Milford Haven. She remained in unmaintained reserve there until 3.47 when she was handed over for scrapping, work being carried out locally by T. W. Ward Ltd during the rest of the year.

HMS BUXTON H 96 (ex USS EDWARDS, DD 265)

Handed over to the Royal Navy at Halifax 8.10.40, BUXTON arrived at St John's NF 18.10 en route to Devonport, but was then delayed by defects. She returned to Halifax for repair, and it was 3.3.41 before the overworked dockyard completed her. She then made a return passage to Bermuda (delayed there eight days by further defects) and was subsequently employed as a local escort in Canadian waters.

A two months refit at Boston in 8 and 9.41 was followed by brief duty at Halifax prior to escorting troop convoy TC14 to the Clyde, there to join 26th Escort Group on arrival. However, this attachment was brief, as she was taken in hand at Chatham for a major refit in mid 11.41 which lasted until the end of 2.42. Trials, work up (during which she went aground) and subsequent repairs occupied the ship until the end of 5.42, when she joined B6 Group based at Liverpool. While with B6, BUXTON escorted convoys and individual, important, ships in the Atlantic until in 8.43 she was ordered to Halifax to join the RCN Western Local Escort Force based on that port.

The WLEF was responsible for escort work between the port of New York, Halifax, and the Western Ocean Meeting Point east of St John's NF. BUXTON remained with WLEF for a year, interspersed with a Boston refit from 12.42 to 3.43, and increasing defect periods at Halifax. Finally in 8.43, the end of operational service came when BUXTON was transferred to the RCN for use as a static training ship, first at Halifax and later at Digby. BUXTON paid off from this mundane but important service 16.1.45 and was finally sold by the RCN for scrap 21.3.46 after a useful, if undistinguished, career spent largely distant from British waters.

Showing her well worn paintwork, BUXTON is seen here while serving with B6 Escort Group. 286 radar at the foremasthead, 271 radar atop the bridge, beam 4" guns replaced by 20 mm Oerliken with two further singles sited abeam the searchlight further aft. The triple centreline torpedo tube mounting is abaft the searchlight; note the very restricted working space for the two after depth charge throwers and the two rails. The rising sheer line shows up well in this picture, note also the propeller guards raised to deck level and the RN 12 pdr HA in X position   *Admiralty*

BUXTON shows badly-marked paintwork, the result of North Atlantic weather. The photograph appears to have been taken on the same occasion as the previous illustration   *Admiralty*

A very interesting, early, photograph taken in Plymouth Sound (The Hoe can be seen in the background) showing CALDWELL in her initial RN state immediately after her first, brief, refit which completed 12.10.40. At this stage the only alterations to the ship are the removal of mainmast and after tubes, even the after 4" gun remains. She has a smart, new, camouflage scheme, but the paintwork has not extended as far as the fourth funnel which still sports the USN Efficiency 'E'. The gun visible against the second funnel is a 0.5" machine gun, not a 20 mm Oerlikon as might be thought   *Imperial War Museum*

HMS CALDWELL I 20 (ex USS HALE, DD 133)

One of the first flotilla to be transferred, CALDWELL commissioned at Halifax 9.9.40 and had a very brief refit at Devonport 28.9 to 12.10. Further repairs were needed at Liverpool prior to her joining 17th Flotilla of Western Approaches Command, nevertheless she was still one of the first of her class operational and sailed with convoy OB233 on 23.10.

Transferred to 5th Escort Group in 12.40, weather damage necessitated repair at Liverpool throughout 1.41, and it seems that she may also have had major crew changes at this time as she then worked up at Tobermory before departing with convoy OB284 on 10.2. CALDWELL continued with 5th EG, despite a long refit at Cardiff 6.6 to 21.8.41, until mid 2.42.

When the submarine war spread to the American East Coast, CALDWELL was one of the ships sent to re-inforce the RCN to form the Western Local Escort Force, arriving at St Johns NF 21.2.42. After a brief spell on the Halifax/St John's route, she transferred to escorting tankers between Halifax and Aruba, until sent to Boston for refit 3.6.42. On completion, the Halifax/St John's route was resumed, CALDWELL being fortunate enough to sustain only minor damage when in collision with *AQUITANIA* 14.8.42. She was not so lucky on 18.1 of that year, during one of the worst winters of the war. Weather damage was so severe on that date that CALDWELL drifted for three days before being taken in tow by WANDERER, and did not make St John's until Christmas Eve. The sight of that small port must have been a welcome Christmas gift for her company.

Unable to be repaired by St John's limited facilities, CALDWELL was then towed south to Boston, arriving 28.1.43 via Halifax, and remained under repair until 1.5. WLEF service then recommenced until 12.43 when, in company with other ships of the class, CALDWELL returned to the UK via the Azores arriving on the Tyne 29.12.43 to go into reserve. Surplus even to auxiliary needs, she lay there until listed for disposal 20.3.45, finally arriving at Granton 7.6.45 to be broken up.

CAMERON was the least fortunate of the fifty ships transferred, never actually entering operational service. She is shown here blown off the blocks in dock at Portsmouth and burnt out. Though salved she never recommissioned   *Admiralty, courtesy D. K. Brown*

HMS CAMERON I 05 (ex USS WELLES, DD 257)

Commissioned at Halifax 9.9.40 as one of the first transfers, CAMERON did not arrive at Belfast on passage from Canada until 7.11. Quite what delayed her passage is not known, probably defects arising after transfer.

Unlike the majority of the TOWNs, CAMERON was sent for refit to Portsmouth, work commencing there on 20.11. On 5.12, during an air raid, she was hit, set on fire and blown off the blocks in No 8 dock. The dock partially flooded as a result of the fire fighting and the ship was not salved until 23.2.41.

Reckoned by the USN to be the worst damaged but surviving destroyer available, she was extensively surveyed to ascertain how the hull and machinery reacted to major explosion. Later still she was used for further shock trials and also for damage control investigation and instruction.

In some records she is shown as having a reduced boiler capacity; it may possibly have been hoped to rebuild her as a Long Range Escort, but quite certainly this was never put in hand. Discarded, she was listed for disposal 5.10.43, but was not removed from Portsmouth until 11.44 when the tug *OWL* towed her to Falmouth, arriving 26.11. She was handed over to T. W. Ward Ltd for scrapping on 1.12.

CAMPBELTOWN seen wedged into the caisson of the Normandie Lock, St Nazaire, very shortly before she exploded. The major shell damage to her port side in way of the messdecks can be clearly seen, similarly the 12pdr HA on the forecastle in lieu of a 4", and the altered fore funnels, all designed to simulate a MOWE class torpedo boat at night

German, via Admiralty

HMS CAMPBELTOWN I 42 (ex USS BUCHANAN, DD 131)

Commissioned at Halifax as one of the first transfers, CAMPBELTOWN received by far the greatest publicity of all the class owing to the circumstances of her end.

CAMPBELTOWN arrived at Devonport 29.9.40 and refitted there to 1.11; a collision with *RISOY* the following day while on trials put her into dockyard hands at Liverpool until 24.11. The ship then joined 17th Flotilla, Western Approaches Command, but yet another collision this time with *COMUS* on 3.12 involved her in further repairs until 28.3.41. During this period, she appears to have had a Polish contingent on board, whether for training or with the intent to man the ship is not clear.

On completion of repairs, CAMPBELTOWN became Dutch manned and the photograph opposite shows her under the Netherlands Ensign, and with an oddly shortened fourth funnel, the only known case of such an alteration. Between 4 and late 9.41 CAMPBELTOWN served with 7th Escort Group apart from one repair period from 9.6 to 3.7. At one stage, the Dutch Government wished to rename the ship MIDDELBURG, but the request was refused as this would have broken the system of twin town naming.

In late 9.41, CAMPBELTOWN reverted to British manning, and after working up with her new crew, joined 27th Escort Group for the West African convoy route. Defects and subsequent repairs kept her in dockyard hands at Devonport from late 1.42, and during this period she was selected as an expendable vessel for use in a raid on the French coast.

CAMPBELTOWN, with an oddly cut down fourth funnel, under Dutch colours
courtesy Sikorski Polish Museum

The port of St Nazaire possessed, in the Normandie Lock built for the liner of that name, the only drydock on the Atlantic coast capable of accepting TIRPITZ. It was decided, therefore, that the destruction of that dock would greatly reduce the possibility of TIRPITZ attempting to operate in the Atlantic and accordingly a combined assault on the area was planned. The intent was to ram the caisson of the Lock with a vessel carrying a large demolition charge (CAMPBELTOWN), to torpedo the gates of a second lock, and to land demolition parties to deal with shore pumping arrangements etc, the whole operation resulting in the effective destruction of the port facilities from a naval point of view.

CAMPBELTOWN underwent a final refit at Devonport during which she lost her third and fourth funnels. The two remaining were altered in diameter and given raked tops, and a 12pdr HA was mounted on the forecastle. The intention was to simulate a MOWE class torpedo boat, some of which were based at St Nazaire. Forward in the ship twenty four depth charges were sealed into the hull to provide the demolition charge, and all other armament, stores etc were removed to lighten the ship. Light armour protection was fitted on the bridge and upper deck for the crew and embarked Commandos, and a number of hand worked 20 mm provided to give covering fire.

In this guise, accompanied by a number of launches and MTBs and provided with the night challenges and replies courtesy of Bletchley Park and Ultra decrypts, CAMPBELTOWN approached St Nazaire during the night of 28/29.3.42, and succeeded in lodging herself in the caisson of the lock. The time fuzes of the charge did not operate as planned and, in the aftermath of the raid, the ship was photographed from varying angles and visited by a large number of German personnel. The first photograph, one of a sequence, shows a substantial party of 'goofers' on the forecastle and the adjacent dockside. These did not remain for long, nor do they seem to have made a proper inspection below decks for, at 1135 local time, CAMPBELTOWN exploded. The result was inevitable, with the lock empty and half tide outside, the caisson was damaged and forced open. It and the wreck of CAMPBELTOWN were swept into the lock by a tidal wave, and very substantial casualties inflicted on the personnel around.

Eventually, the Germans sealed the lock with a sand wall with the intent of commencing repair; the photograph overleaf shows the wrecked CAMPBELTOWN (fore end towards the camera), the dock strewn with NORMANDIE's docking blocks, the ruined caisson at the right rear of the lock and the sand wall sealing all.

CAMPBELTOWN, the aftermath   German, courtesy Naval Historical Branch

A good view of CASTLETON in the full Stage 2 condition, complete with rebuilt bridge. She is storing from auxiliaries alongside, probably in the Clyde
Imperial War Museum

HMS CASTLETON I 23 (ex USS AARON WARD, DD 132)

CASTLETON commissioned at Halifax 9.9.40 and after refit at Devonport was one of the first ships to enter service, on 9.10, joining 17th Flotilla of Western Approaches at Liverpool. CASTLETON was also early into action, taking survivors from *DAYDAWN* and *VICTORIA* when they were sunk in convoy OB244. Two collisions, on 1 and 3.12, sent CASTLETON to Portsmouth for repair and a small refit, Stage 1 alterations being put in hand.

The Portsmouth refit was somewhat prolonged, as the ship received air raid damage on 18.1.41, but repair was completed and she worked up in the Dartmouth area, completing 7.3.41 to join 1st Minelaying Squadron at Kyle of Lochalsh. Here she escorted mining sorties and also acted as local A/S escort for special convoys. She suffered some damage in collision with the minelayer AGAMEMNON 27.3.41, and repaired on the Clyde between 2.4 and 1.6.

Returning to duty with the Squadron, escort work continued, mainly with the Icelandic ferry convoys, during one of which she had the misfortune to have one of her onboard scuttling charges explode. While she was able to continue with the convoy, repairs were needed and were carried out at Newport, Mon. from late 11.41 to 4.42.

Returning to Kyle of Lochalsh on completion of repairs, the usual routine of escort duty was interrupted when CASTLETON was despatched to the aid of an Icelandic trawler. On 20.8 an American flying boat surprised and attacked U464 south east of Iceland. Caught on the surface, the submarine was damaged and unable to dive and, judging that surface ships would soon arrive, scuttled herself close to an Icelandic trawler. 52 crew members of U464 got onboard, but CASTLETON and NEWARK arrived before they were able to take over the ship and endeavour to make a break for Norway. In 9.42 also, CASTLETON spent some days as escort for the diving tender TEDWORTH which was engaged in salvage operations on the *BARRANCA*.

CASTLETON detached from the Minelaying Squadron for refit at Cardiff in 12.42 and on completion in 3.43 joined Rosyth Command as the Minelaying Squadron had been disbanded. Nevertheless, she still escorted five final mining sorties by individual ships and then continued to escort the Icelandic ferry convoys. Here, again, she was involved in the collection of U boat survivors, picking up members of the crew of U489 on 4.8.43. Later in 1943 CASTLETON was engaged as an Air Target Ship, but in 1.44 she became part of the Rosyth Escort Force and operated with East Coast convoys as an escort.

By late 1944, sufficient escorts were available to release the old ship, and in 10.44 she reverted to Air Target duty until 13.3.45 when she paid off to lay up at Grangemouth and await disposal. Handed over for scrapping 4.3.47, she remained in her Grangemouth berth until towed to Bo'ness where she arrived 2.1.48 to be broken up by P. & W. MacLellan Ltd.

In 1950, the ship's bell was presented to the town of Castleton, Vermont as a gesture of the Royal Navy's appreciation.

Not the clearest of photographs of CHARLESTOWN, but shows the removal of the beam 4" guns and their replacement by single 20 mm, which are also fitted aft by the small mainmast; and the centreline torpedo tubes. 271 radar tops the bridge, probably 286 at the masthead   *Admiralty*

HMS CHARLESTOWN I 21 (ex USS ABBOT, DD 184)

CHARLESTOWN was somewhat delayed in entering service as, although transferred at Halifax 23.9.40 and refitted at Devonport completing 4.11, subsequent defects delayed her arrival at Kyle of Lochalsh to join 17th Division until 6.1.41, the unit with which she was to serve until 2.43.

In addition to escorting 1st Minelaying Squadron in its work on the Northern Barrage, the ship was also used extensively to cover the Icelandic Ferry convoys, and also served as a local escort for major troop convoys sailing from the Clyde.

CHARLESTOWN refitted, with BEVERLEY, at Palmers on Tyneside during 4 and 5.41, and again refitted at Grimsby from mid 11.41. This refit was prolonged as she was rammed by *MARPLE* while alongside, and repairs did not complete until 20.2.42. After further service, again often with the Icelandic convoys, CHARLESTOWN went for refit at Newport, Mon. in late 10.42, transferring to Cardiff when she hit the dockside while leaving for trials; repairs in fact lasted until 2.43.

Following the Newport refit and subsequent work up at Tobermory CHARLESTOWN came under the command of Admiral Commanding Orkney and Shetland until 8.43, the Minelaying Squadron having disbanded. Repairs were then needed which were done at Belfast, and in 10.43 CHARLESTOWN transferred to Rosyth Command for duty on the East Coast convoy route. While so serving, CHARLESTOWN collided with FLORIZEL off Harwich on 10.12.44. The damage incurred, the age and condition of the ship, and the number of escorts now available all combined to decide that no further effort would be expended and CHARLESTOWN was paid off in her damaged state and laid up at Grangemouth. She passed to the control of British Iron & Steel Corporation on 4.3.47, and arrived at Sunderland in tow on 3.12.48 to be broken up by Thos Young & Sons Ltd.

Taken after her London refit, this photograph shows CHELSEA prior to sailing to Canada and quite possibly in the Thames on her way to work up. She is in the full Stage 2 condition complete with Hedgehog forward of the extended bridge, 271 and 291 radars, 20 mm in the beam 4" position and further aft, and with a triple centreline torpedo tube mounting　　　　　　　　　　　　　　　*Imperial War Museum*

HMS CHELSEA I 35 (ex USS CROWNINSHIELD, DD 134)

One of the first batch to transfer at Halifax, CHELSEA was also one of the longest serving. She arrived at Devonport for refit 28.9.40, and joined 17th Flotilla at Liverpool on 12.10. Further defects were made good at Liverpool between 4.11 and 6.12, and CHELSEA then joined 6th Escort Group serving on both the Atlantic and Gibraltar convoy routes.

In 9.41 CHELSEA collided with *CANNING* and, after repair, again with the same ship on 1.11, this time with only minor damage. However, a third collision with an unknown ship on 16.11 sent her back to the repairers for a month. On completion enough defects accumulated by 2.42 to send her to London for a major repair and refit.

On completion of post refit work up, CHELSEA went to Canada to serve in the Western Local Escort Force. Unusually (for a TOWN) she appears to have had only two repair periods (each of four weeks) between 9.42 and 12.43, both at New York City. Either the London repairers did an excellent job, or the surviving records are incomplete.

DZERKI in Russian service　　　　　　　　　　　　　　　*courtesy Naval Museum, Leningrad*

In 12.43, in common with the other RN TOWNs of WLEF, CHELSEA sailed from St John's NF 15.12 for the UK via the Azores to pay off and lay up in reserve. This however, was not the end of her service as she was selected for transfer to the Russian Northern Fleet in mid 1944. Refitted by Palmers on Tyneside from 14.2 to 6.3 and again from 3 to 9.5, CHELSEA became DZERKI on 16.7 and was steamed to Kola with her sisters and the battleship ARCHANGELSK during the passage of JW59, sailing 15.8.

During passage, enthusiasm, inexperience and Arctic ASDIC conditions provoked a surfeit of 'non sub' contacts, the Russians reporting 62 contacts, one sinking and three probables. Cold fact, unfortunately, bears out none of these claims after post war research into German records, but the ship cannot be accused of inactivity.

Service with the Northern Fleet followed, and the ship was again claimed to be in action 9.12.44, but without confirmation that she took any part in the loss of U387. DZERKI was present when DYATELNYI was sunk, and was able to pick up eight survivors. Other operations were carried out up to 5.45, principally in the White Sea.

DZERKI returned to Britain and was formally handed back to the RN at Rosyth on 24.6.49. At once declared for disposal, she passed to BISCo 12.7 and arrived at Bo'ness 29.7 for scrapping by P. & W. MacLellan Ltd.

Shown here on completion of her refit at Hull, CHESTERFIELD is fully equipped as a Stage 2 North Atlantic escort. Note Hedgehog forward of the rebuilt bridge, which carries 271 radar, 20 mm in the beam gun positions, centreline torpedo tubes and, well aft, HF/DF on its tall mainmast   *Admiralty*

HMS CHESTERFIELD I 28 (ex USS WELBORN C WOOD, DD 195)

One of the first transfers, on 9.9.40, CHESTERFIELD had a somewhat chequered start to her British career, colliding with CHURCHILL on 10.9. After sailing for Britain, she arrived at St John's with defects that required her return to Halifax. Setting forth once more, she arrived at St John's 22.10, only to be quarantined with a case of diptheria onboard, so that she did not arrive at Devonport until 22.11.40.

Unusually for a TOWN, CHESTERFIELD's refit was at Chatham and lasted from 26.11 to 25.1.41, with trials at Devonport in the following days. Allocated to 11th Escort Group she was, finally, able to enter operational service on 27.2, despite a collision with the submarine H32 on that date.

In mid 4.41 the Group moved base from Liverpool to Iceland, immediately followed by CHESTERFIELD being shifted to 3rd Escort Group also based there. Duty with mid Atlantic convoys and on the Denmark Strait patrol, took its toll of an old ship and repair on the Clyde throughout 5.41 was needed. By mid 6.41 CHESTERFIELD had transferred to Newfoundland Escort Force in 18th Escort Group, again changing to 23rd Escort Group in 7.41. All these Groups were committed to North Atlantic escort work.

On 6.9 CHESTERFIELD was in collision with BURNHAM, fortunately without serious damage to either ship, and it was not until 6.10 that CHESTERFIELD arrived at Portsmouth for a refit lasting until 17.1.42.

Following refit and work up, CHESTERFIELD joined 26th Escort Group for two Atlantic convoys, but then needed further attention from Clydeside repairers between 29.3 and 23.6.42. She next became part of B7 Group, but only briefly as after only two return passages to Canada and a brief period with convoy WS22, CHESTERFIELD arrived at Hull for a two month refit in 10.42. The ship completed with a comprehensive A/S fit for North Atlantic work and it is unfortunate therefore that after only one return crossing shallow set depth charges damaged the ship whilst with convoy HX222. CHESTERFIELD thereafter lay under repair from mid 2.43 until 11.43, nominally part of Western Approaches Command, until allocated to Rosyth Command for target duty.

Even in the role of an Air Target Ship, CHESTERFIELD seems to have been dogged by misfortune, for she was again laid up, this time at Dundee, for repairs from late 3.44 until 11.44. At this point, the decision was taken not to waste further resources and CHESTERFIELD paid off on 15.1.45 to lay up at Rosyth, remaining there until towed to Dunston on Tyne where she arrived 3.12.48 to be broken up by Clayton & Davie Ltd.

Shown in her final appearance in British service, with Hedgehog forward of an extended bridge topped by 271 radar, single 20 mm in the beam positions, abaft the fourth funnel and in bandstands by the searchlight tower, centreline torpedo tubes, and HF/DF on its tall mast forward of the 12pdr   *Admiralty*

HMS CHURCHILL I 45 (ex USS HERNDON, DD 198)

HMS CHURCHILL was ostensibly named for a small village, and a similarly named town in the USA, though it is noteworthy that the present ship of the name (the SSN) claims the statesman; in any event the ship was commissioned at Halifax 9.9.40. Delayed at Halifax repairing collision damage with CHESTERFIELD, she arrived at Devonport 17.11 having searched for survivors of JERVIS BAY while on passage. She completed refit in time to provide part of the initial escort for troop convoy WS5B in mid 1.41.

Initially based in Liverpool with 3rd Escort Group, she then transferred to Iceland and finally Newfoundland with 18th Escort Group, trans Atlantic convoy being the duty of all three assignments. A long repair commencing in 9.41 at Liverpool and completing at Dundee in 1.42 preceded transfer to B5 Group. This Group was one of a number of British ships assigned to duty with the USN in the West Indies to assist when the USN was unable to cope with the scale of attack, and CHURCHILL so served until taken in hand for refit at Charleston SC in late 9.42.

On completion of her US refit, CHURCHILL passed to Canadian control joining C4 Group and again operating in the North Atlantic except for two fast convoys to and from Algiers.

As with the majority of the class, age and defects caused retirement to reserve and CHURCHILL duly laid up on Tyneside in 2.44.

However, the need to lend ships to Russia brought CHURCHILL back into service and after refit she became DYATELNYI on 30.5.44. In company with other ships also loaned, she steamed to Kola and the Northern Fleet during the passage of convoy JW59.

Employed as an escort in the far North, distinction was achieved as the last war loss of the class, DYATELNYI being torpedoed and sunk by U956 on 16.1.45 while escorting a White Sea convoy; the only one of the transferred destroyers to be lost.

Two views of HMS CHURCHILL, presumably taken during her service in the Caribbean under USN control
United States Navy

Clare

CLARE photographed in Plymouth Sound immediately after completion of her conversion to a Long Range Escort in 10.41

In the course of conversion, the two forward boilers and their funnels have been removed (the space being utilised to provide an additional 80 tons oil fuel stowage, messdecks, stores, etc.) The bridge has been rebuilt in accordance with British destroyer practice (note that the face is angled, not flat as the photograph implies) and the whole superstructure has been extended aft to the midships deckhouse. 271 radar is fitted above the bridge, the beam 4" guns have been replaced (unusually) by single 2pdr and single 20 mm appear in a bandstand abaft the remaining funnels. The torpedo tubes have been reduced to a triple centreline mounting. Hedgehog is not yet fitted; another twelve months were to pass before this became available   Admiralty

HMS CLARE I 14 (ex USS ABEL P UPSHUR, DD 193)

CLARE was an early transfer, on 9.9.40, and refitted at Devonport to join 17th Flotilla of Western Approaches on 9.10, one of the first TOWNs to be operational. She was very soon overtaken by defects, however, being taken in hand at Liverpool on 17.11. She was then transferred to Portsmouth for further work and, after trials and a collision with *PETERTON* on 21.2.41, it was decided to convert her to a Long Range Escort at Devonport, the work lasting from 22.2.41 to 14.10.41. Thus it was more than thirteen months after transfer before she became fully operational in the form shown in the illustrations.

With the increased range provided by her refit, CLARE joined 41st Escort Group operating on the new OS convoy route to Freetown, and continued escorting these convoys and the return SL series until their suspension due to the forthcoming North African invasion (Operation TORCH). 41st EG took a full part in escorting the convoys for and following that invasion, until 7.43. CLARE then made an unusual (for a British escort) passage from Gibraltar to the USA escorting a convoy of the GUS series, returning to Britain with convoy UT1 from Argentia to go for refit at Cardiff in 9.43.

While under refit at Cardiff, CLARE suffered a fire onboard so that it was not until 6.44 that she was able to leave the repair yard, and then reduced to Air Target Ship status. In this role she served mainly in the Irish Sea, until paid off in mid 8.45 and laid up at Barrow. Finally allocated for scrap in 1947, CLARE arrived at Troon on 18.2.47 to be broken up by West of Scotland Shipbreaking Co Ltd.

Taken at the same time as the photograph on the previous page, this picture of CLARE shows the substantial alterations made aft as part of the Long Range Escort conversion   *Admiralty*

A mid war photograph of COLUMBIA showing how little the ship had changed since transfer. Just visible is the SW1C radar at the foremasthead, the beam tubes are still mounted, and other than the addition of splinter mats the bridge remains unaltered   *courtesy K. Macpherson*

HMCS COLUMBIA I 49 (ex USS HARADEN, DD 183)

COLUMBIA was one of the TOWNs retained in Canada and manned by the RCN, and she served locally at Halifax until 1.41 when she came to Devonport for a brief refit thereafter joining 4th Escort Group until mid 1941.

On the formation of Newfoundland Command, COLUMBIA's low radius and Canadian crew naturally led to her return to Canadian waters, and she was thereafter based at Halifax.

Like all her sisters, she suffered increasingly from defects brought on by age, the inexperience of many Canadian personnel and the overtaxed base facilities available in Canada. She did well to remain in service until 1944, but the end came when she struck a cliff at Moreton Bay, Newfoundland on 25.2. Technically, she did not ground, as she never touched bottom, but the impact crushed the ship's bows and she was towed to St John's NF where she lay unrepaired until 7.1944. Then, minus her damaged bows, she was hulked at Liverpool NS as a static fuel and ammunition depot for ships under refit. Paid off from this duty 12.6.45, the hulk was sold for scrap 7.8.45.

COLUMBIA, minus her bows, lying as a hulk at Livepool, N.S.   *R.C.N.*

*GEORGETOWN in Stage 2 condition, complete with Hedgehog but prior to the bridge alterations illustrated
opposite*
Admiralty

HMS GEORGETOWN I 40 (ex USS MADDOX, DD 168)

GEORGETOWN transferred at Halifax 23.9.40 and sailed for Britain six days later, but a collision with
HAMILTON at St John's NF returned her to Halifax for repair and she did not finally arrive at Devonport until
13.11.40. Completing a brief refit there, she worked up at Scapa Flow until 17.12, and then joined 4th Escort
Group.

A collision with an unknown ship on 26.2.41 sent her to the Tyne for repair in early 6.41, followed by more
work on Clydeside until mid 7.41. On completion she transferred to 3rd Escort Group and returned to North
Atlantic escort work.

GEORGETOWN transferred again to 27th Escort Group in 9.41, and commenced her Stage 2 refit on the
Clyde in mid 11.41. Completion was delayed by a boiler room fire on 13.12 and it was mid 4.42 before she
was ready for service. Her first escort duty was to escort convoy WS18, and then the carrier EAGLE and USS
WASP en route to Gibraltar for Operation BOWERY (transfer of Spitfires to Malta) after which she returned
to the Clyde for a further four weeks repair.

In 6.42 GEORGETOWN joined the Special Escort Division of the Greenock force, covering two WS troop
convoys, a homeward bound HG convoy and a minelaying sortie. She was then allocated to support the RCN
and sailed to join the Western Local Escort Force based at Halifax where she saw the balance of her active
service in British hands. She refitted at Charleston SC between 3.43 and 5.43, and in 11.43 returned to Britain
via the Azores to lay up in reserve at Hartlepool.

The ship was one of the destroyers selected for loan to Russia and, after refit at Middle Docks, Tyneside,
was transferred as ZHOSTKI during 8.44, to join the Northern Fleet. She was returned in tow from Murmansk
to Rosyth and handed over on 9.9.52, passing at once to the shipbreakers and arriving at Inverkeithing on
16.9 to be broken up by T. W. Ward Ltd.

Two views of GEORGETOWN after the refit in South Carolina   USN

A very clear illustration of the deck layout of a TOWN after Stage 2 refit. This is GEORGETOWN shortly after an American refit in 5.43. Note the very limited space aft with the depth charge rails sponsored over the counter, the 12 pdr HA on the after superstructure, a new mainmast for the HF/DF aerial, and centreline triple torpedo tubes   USN

Further photographs of GEORGETOWN taken after her refit at Charleston, SC. Clearly visible is the Hedgehog forward of the rebuilt bridge. 20 mm Oerlikons can be seen in the 4" beam positions and further aft, centreline torpedo tubes and HF/DF   *USN*

Other than the removal of the mainmast, after 4" and 3" guns, and tubes, and the cropping of the three after funnels, HAMILTON is virtually unchanged from the date of handover. SW1C is carried at the foremasthead
courtesy K. Macpherson

HMCS HAMILTON I 24 (ex USS KALK, DD 170)

HAMILTON had a somewhat chequered start to her career; manned by the Royal Navy, she collided with GEORGETOWN at St John's NF on 4.10.40 and had to return to Halifax for repair. Haste in undocking her on 25.10 caused further serious damage so that she was paid off and her crew used to man other ships of the class. On completion of repair, it was decided to transfer her to the RCN as the seventh TOWN unit, but she retained her British name.

An intriguing picture of HAMILTON, still carrying a searchlight on her bridge, whose camouflage appears to have been "retouched" somewhat in the area of the bridge and aft
Imperial War Museum

HAMILTON was employed entirely on the Eastern seaboard, commencing on 12.7.41; with increasing repair problems she was retired from active service in 8.43 and thereafter employed in the Bay of Fundy area as a training ship, starting in 12.43, until the end of the war.

Finally paid off 8.6.45, HAMILTON was sold to Frankel Bros acting as agents for Boston Iron & Metal Co. Together with ST FRANCIS she left Sydney NS in tow of *FOUNDATION SECURITY* for Boston and the breakers yard. At this point records become unclear, the tow was in collision with *WINDING GULF* and parted, one of the two hulks was taken in tow by USCGC HORNBEAM and beached as a total loss 14.7.45. It is believed that this was, in fact, ST FRANCIS, but at least one RCN report indicates HAMILTON while admitting the lack of firm evidence. In any event, one flush deck wreck lies off Sakonnet Point, Rhode Island.

LANCASTER taken fairly early in her service, still in Stage 1 condition. 286 radar at the masthead and the absence of 271 indicates a date between 9.41 and late 1942   Admiralty

HMS LANCASTER G 05 (ex USS PHILIP, DD 76)

LANCASTER commissioned at Halifax 23.10.40, and was one of the few ships not to refit at Devonport, arriving at Portsmouth 26.11. Completing refit 11.1.41, LANCASTER worked up at Scapa Flow prior to joining 1st Minelaying Squadron at Kyle of Lochalsh. She escorted several minelaying sorties, and the four inaugural convoys of the Icelandic ferry service (DS/SD convoys), prior to arriving on Humberside for her Stage 2 refit from 6 to 9.41. LANCASTER returned to her duty and continued until the end of 1942, with one break for refit at Newport Mon, 4 to 6.42. In 9.42 LANCASTER escorted shipping to and from Gibraltar in connection with the North African invasion, being released for refit at Belfast in 1.43. Completed and worked up at Tobermory in 5.43, LANCASTER escorted four final minelaying sorties before transferring to Rosyth Command when the Minelaying Squadron paid off.

After transfer to Rosyth, LANCASTER was employed on the East Coast convoy route, being damaged in collision with the Swedish *HEDERA* 25.1.44, and involved in rescue operations when ROCKINGHAM foundered off Aberdeen after striking a British mine.

Allocated to Air Target Service in 2.45, the consequent refit was cancelled at the end of the war and the ship went into reserve unaltered, finally arriving at Blyth 30.5.47 to be broken up by Hughes Bolckow Shipbreaking Co. Ltd.

Leamington

An early photograph of LEAMINGTON in Stage 1 state, apparently closing a fellow escort. An interesting comparison with the last photograph in the publication
Admiralty

HMS LEAMINGTON G 19 (ex USS TWIGGS, DD 127)

After transfer at Halifax 23.10.40, LEAMINGTON refitted at Devonport 15.11 to 29.11, briefly escorted convoy SL56 and then worked up at Scapa Flow from 15.12 to 5.1.41 prior to joining 2nd Escort Group for North Atlantic work.

LEAMINGTON's extensive convoy escort duty was interrupted when she collided with, and sank *THYRA* on 27.5.41 requiring repair at Liverpool to mid 7.41. She rejoined her Group and was heavily involved in the fighting around convoy SC42, during which she shared the sinking of U207 on 11.9.41 with VETERAN.

In 2.42 LEAMINGTON commenced escorting troop convoys of the AT, TA and WS series in the UK approaches; whilst so covering WS17 she scored her second success by sinking U587 on 27.3.42. LEAMINGTON continued with her special escort task until 6.42, when she formed part of the UK to Iceland escort for PQ17, followed by covering a minelaying sortie by 1st Minelaying Squadron. She then went to long refit at Hartlepool from 7 to 11.42 followed by transfer to Halifax to serve with the RCN in the Western Local Escort Force, arriving at Halifax in 1.43.

LEAMINGTON suffered two collisions while operating from Halifax, with USS ALBATROSS which put her under repair from 15.4 to 3.6 and a less serious brush with *MORTIMER,* the repair for which did not commence until late 6.43 at Norfolk, Va, continuing to 10.43.

Like a number of her sisters in the WLEF, LEAMINGTON returned to Britain in 12.43, and laid up in reserve in 2.44. Refitted and transferred to Russia as ZHGUCHI 16.7.44, she served with the Northern Fleet, and did not return to Rosyth until 15.11.50. Laid up and transferred to BISCo for scrapping in 7.51, she was then hired as a 'film extra', finally arriving at Newport, Mon 3.12.51 to be broken up by J. Cashmore & Sons Ltd. A brief account of her days as a film star, and a photograph of her in that role, appear as the endpiece to this book.

One of the first six of the flush deckers to be transferred, LEEDS was one of two three funnelled ships which came to the Royal Navy
The photograph shows the replacement of A gun by two single 2pdrs, the retention of the beam and after guns (US 3"/50 not 4") the absence of torpedo tubes, and the fitting of two single 20 mm in bandstands aft. 286 radar and a VHF aerial are carried at the masthead, the upper bridge is enlarged but still only splinter mat protected
Admiralty

HMS LEEDS G 27 (ex USS CONNER, DD 72)

LEEDS and her sister LUDLOW were two of the six earliest TOWN class built, and were amongst the most unusual. Apart from being three stackers (of which the RN got two) the armament differed from other flush deckers, as did the form of the stern; in the case of LEEDS and LUDLOW they also had unusual engines, direct drive turbines to three rather than two shafts, with a cruising turbine on the centre shaft. This arrangement, admitted by the USN to be unusual and outdated in 1916, must have sorely puzzled their steaming crews at Halifax, and probably resulted in LEEDS protracted refit at Devonport from 17.11.40 to 2.3.41.

Further re-armament later in her career increased the 20 mm fit to five weapons, probably the most effective guns onboard as the ship was employed entirely on the East coast convoy route for the whole of her service.

Examining the ship's movements appears to indicate a horrific amount of time in dockyard hands; closer search shows that in fact it comprised a more or less monthly 'in hand' for defects, just what was needed to keep such an unusual ship running. Finally paid off at Grangemouth 10.4.45, LEEDS passed to BISCo 4.3.47 and arrived at Grays, Essex 19.1.49 to be broken up by T. W. Ward Ltd.

LEEDS, taken in 1942. This photograph clearly shows the different hull form aft compared with the usual TOWN. The long barrelled 3"/50 cal guns can be seen aft and in the wing positions close to the centre funnel. No torpedo tubes remain, and note the lack of depth charge equipment, LEEDS was operating on the East Coast where they were not needed   *Admiralty*

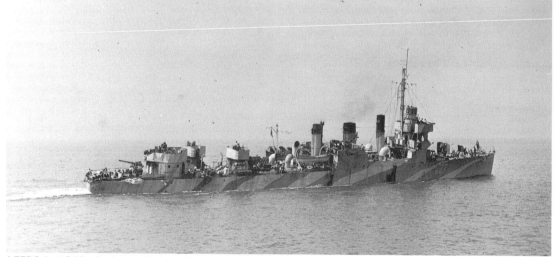

LEEDS in 1943, the beam 3" have been replaced by the 2 pdrs from the forecastle, where a 12 pdr is now mounted. 20 mm Oerlikon appear aft. Depth charge equipment has been replaced since the preceding photograph was taken   *Admiralty*

LEEDS; a peaceful alongside view, probably at Rosyth, showing the altered bridge structure and the British 12 pdr forward. A late photograph, possibly taken early in 1945   *Admiralty*

LEWES was still serving with the Rosyth Escort Force at the time of this photograph (10.42). The replacement of the forward gun by two single 2pdrs is clearly shown, as is the unusually shaped upper bridge. Only 286 radar and VHF appear to be fitted at this time

Admiralty

HMS LEWES G 68 (ex USS CONWAY, ex USS CRAVEN, DD 70)

LEWES was 'odd' in the TOWN class for a number of reasons. Prior to her transfer she had, like ST MARYS, been stricken from the USN list of ships and her name allocated to new construction. Accordingly, when the time came to commission her prior to transfer, a new name had to be allocated for the short period when she was again in commission; researchers will not easily therefore find a USS CONWAY in the lists of ships. LEWES was also unusual in that she was the only four funnelled TOWN to mount 3"/50cal guns instead of 4", a suit that she shared with the two three stackers LEEDS and LUDLOW. Finally, as will be seen as her story is told, she became the furthest travelled of the TOWNs.

LEWES arrived at Devonport 17.11.40 for refit which lasted until 28.3.41, like LEEDS a symptom of her age and early design. She also had the misfortune to be bombed during an air raid on Devonport on 22.4.41, while still in the yard, so that she did not finally enter service with Rosyth Command until 2.42, the last TOWN to become fully operational.

After only ten months of escort work on the East Coast, LEWES refitted on the Humber as an Air Target Ship until 3.43, whereon she was ordered to join the South Atlantic Command based on Capetown. She went out with troop convoy WS29, and other than for one inexplicable passage to Casablanca and back in 1/2.44, remained on station in the target role.

In 8.44, the East Indies Fleet having at last attained a reasonable carrier strength and local Air Stations. the need arose for an Air Target Ship in Ceylon. LEWES was duly ordered East to her new Station, where she actually saw operational service, being used for escort to at least one supply convoy from Ceylon to Addu Atoll in 9.44.

In 1945, the needs of war caused yet another move further east. The newly formed British Pacific Fleet had set up training Air Stations in Australia, and LEWES was ordered to Sydney NSW to operate as a target for them. She duly sailed from Trincomalee to Fremantle escorting the depot ship TYNE, and then went onward to her new post where she served out the war.

The old ship outlived all her sisters in British service, not paying off until 11.45 at Sydney NSW where, nominally passed to BISCo for disposal, she was stripped of valuable scrap and the hull scuttled off Sydney 25.5.46.

LEWES in her East Coast escort form, the long barrelled 3" aft and amidships are very prominent. Unlike her half sisters LEEDS and LUDLOW on the same duty, she has retained her depth charge armament, the rails and throwers can be seen quite clearly

Admiralty

An extremely clear view of LINCOLN out of Charleston SC after refit. Although not evident in this view, she is in fact Norwegian manned. 291 radar tops the foremast and 271 radar the altered bridge, with Hedgehog forward of it. Centreline torpedo tubes and 20 mm abeam the funnels complete the Stage 2 refit
Admiralty

HMS LINCOLN G 42 (ex USS YARNALL, DD 143)

LINCOLN was destined to serve under three flags when she transferred at Halifax on 23.10.40. Following her arrival at Devonport 15.11, she briefly refitted until 30.11, and then joined 1st Escort Group to operate in the Eastern Atlantic until 9.41. During this time she was involved in the rescue of survivors from the Armed Merchant Cruiser COMORIN when that ship burnt out and sank 6.4.41.

LINCOLN underwent a protracted refit on the Thames from 9.41 to 3.42, after which she was manned by the Royal Norwegian Navy and allocated to serve with the RCN based on Halifax in the WLEF. Whilst serving at Halifax, LINCOLN refitted at Charleston SC, and also reverted to British manning. At one point she became a unit of W7 group in the short lived Western Support Force.

Returning to Britain in 12.43, LINCOLN laid up until transferred to her third flag, Russian, on 26.8.44 when she became DRUZHNY. Sailing to Murmansk during the passage of convoy JW60, she served in the Northern Fleet until returned to Britain and the Royal Navy at Rosyth on 24.8.52. She was transferred to the breakers without delay and arrived at Charlestown 3.9.52 to be broken up by Metal Industries Ltd.

A nice clear photograph of LINCOLN wearing Norwegian colours. She is in the Stage 2 state, with close range weapons abeam the funnels and the searchlight tower, centre line torpedo tubes and the usual depth charge throwers and rails aft. Taken in 3.43, she appears to have landed her port boat, perhaps for stability reasons
Admiralty

LUDLOW, seen here in her initial armament layout, similar to her sister LEEDS. The forward 3" has been replaced by two single 2pdr while retaining the beam and after guns. Single 20 mm are fitted in bandstands, and all torpedo tubes have been removed. The half cased funnels, unique to LEEDS and LUDLOW, are accentuated here by the black paint applied above the casing
Admiralty

This, later, photograph shows LUDLOW in her final form. For some unknown reason the forward 2pdrs have been replaced by a 12pdr HA, a somewhat dubious change in view of the East Coast employment. 271 radar has now been added, with 291 and VHF at the masthead. The beam 3" have been replaced by the 2pdrs removed from the forecastle, possibly these are in powered mountings though the photograph does not permit positive identification. 20 mm remain in the bandstands, and the after 3" is retained   **Admiralty**

HMS LUDLOW G 57 (ex USS STOCKTON, DD 73)

Transferred at Halifax 23.10.40, LUDLOW refitted at Devonport 17.9.40 to 1.3.41, a protracted affair like the other older TOWNs. On completion of refit she joined Rosyth Command, in which she served throughout the war escorting East Coast convoys.

Paid off in 5.45, the old ship was stripped at Rosyth and then beached as a target for rocket firing aircraft on 6.6.45. A month later the sunken wreck was passed to BISCo for disposal, but little or no work seems to have been done as her remains may still be seen at low water off Fidra Island in the Forth, the position being 56.03.95N 02.45.85W.

Like LEEDS, LUDLOW was one of only three three funnelled units and had the same unusual stern form, and three shafts with direct drive turbines with a cruising turbine on the centre shaft additionally.

HMS MANSFIELD G 76 (ex USS EVANS, DD 78)

MANSFIELD was handed over at Halifax 23.10.40 and started refit at Devonport a month later. On 16.12 she was transferred to the Royal Norwegian Navy for manning and completed her refit 9.1.41 to join 6th Escort Group at Londonderry, after a brief spell in the Channel.

MANSFIELD suffered a complete engine failure 24.3, being towed home by SALISBURY to repair at Liverpool for ten days. She completed just in time to take part in a Commando raid on Oksfjord 11.4, after which she rejoined her Group, by now based in Iceland.

6th Escort Group returned to Britain in 6.41, and MANSFIELD refitted at Liverpool in 8.41; further work being needed, she moved to Chatham 19.10 and while there the ship paid off 11.2.42 and reverted to the Royal Navy. When the refit was completed 11.5, MANSFIELD went to Tobermory to work up. Whilst there she collided with *BRITISH LADY* and required repair at Liverpool from 6.6 to 10.7 after which she became part of the Liverpool Special Escort Division, making a return passage to Gibraltar.

In 8.42 MANSFIELD was allocated to WLEF under RCN command based at Halifax, later she was to join the Western Support Force in 1.43. She was heavily involved in the critical convoy actions of 3.43 with convoy HX229, landing survivors in the UK. The ship then refitted on the Thames prior to returning to the Western Escort Force as part of unit W7.

Worn out by constant escort work in Atlantic weather, MANSFIELD paid off at Halifax in 11.43. She was offered to the USN as a source of spares for that Service's own flush deckers, but the offer was declined and she therefore went onto the Disposal List on 22.6.44 being sold 24.10 for breaking up.

Photographed approximately 5/6.41, MANSFIELD has not altered greatly since transfer, other than for the loss of the after torpedo tubes, mainmast and after guns and the mounting of a 12 pdr aft. The guns abeam the second funnel are 5" machine guns, not 20 mm as may be supposed   *Admiralty*

If the photograph datestamp of 8.42 is correct, this photograph of MANSFIELD was taken immediately prior to her departure for Canada to join WLEF. 286 and 271 radars are clearly evident as is Hedgehog and the other usual Stage 2 refinements   *Admiralty*

Clearly showing the limited space aft for A/S weapons crews, MONTGOMERY displays all the Stage 2 alterations, plus an additional pair of single 20 mm in bandstands close to the searchlight   Admiralty

HMS MONTGOMERY G 95 (ex USS WICKES, DD 75)

MONTGOMERY commissioned at Halifax 25.10.40 and refitted at Devonport from 20.11, post trials defects delaying work up until Christmas Eve when she arrived at Scapa Flow. Work up was completed on 12.1.41 and she then joined the 7th Escort Group.

With 7th EG, she escorted numerous convoys, rescuing survivors from *SCOTTISH STANDARD* 21.2.41, and sinking the Italian submarine MARCELLO the following day.

Refitted at Barrow to Stage 2 4 to 9.41, MONTGOMERY then joined 4th EG for four convoys before going to refit on the Clyde 7.10 to 25.11.41 prior to joining WLEF at Halifax.

MONTGOMERY commenced her Canadian attachment, arriving at St John's 16.1.42, with a month's refit at Halifax followed by escorting troop convoy NA3 back to the Clyde. In fact, she was not operational on the Canadian coast until 14.3.42, but thereafter she remained there until late 12.43.

MONTGOMERY seems to have had few major problems, as her list of repairs at Halifax are fewer than normal. Transferred to unit W1 in 2.43, and W6 in 3.43, MONTGOMERY concluded her service when she sailed for Britain via Horta at the end of 12.43. On arrival she paid off to reserve on the Tyne, and remained there until declared for disposal 20.3.45, actually arriving at Dunston on Tyne 10.4 to be broken up by Clayton & Davie Ltd.

HMS NEWARK G 08 (ex USS RINGGOLD, DD 89)

NEWARK was another of the TOWNs bedevilled by ill luck at the start of their British service. Transferred at Halifax 26.11.40, and actually commissioned on 5.12, she was in collision at St John's with NEWMARKET and had to repair from 19.12.40 to 29.1.41. After finally sailing for Devonport, she broke down in heavy weather and had to be towed back to St John's. As a result she did not arrive at Devonport until 9.3.41 for refit and, when almost completed, was rammed by VOLUNTEER on 10.4, so that she left Devonport for Belfast needing hull repairs, arriving for these on 18.4. Even now her misfortunes continued, for she was further damaged in the very heavy air raid on Belfast 4/5.5.41; the disruption of work in the yard leading to her not entering operational service until 15.8.41, a very long time since transfer for a ship still far from a modernised state.

A nice clear picture of NEWARK prior to her receiving her new bridge. Otherwise, she has all the refinements shown in the photograph below
Admiralty

NEWARK joined the 17th Destroyer Division attached to 1st Minelaying Squadron at Kyle of Lochalsh, and entered the usual round of minelaying sorties, Icelandic and troop convoy escort duty. She had a long refit from 2.42 to 5.42, followed by a Tobermory work up prior to rejoining her old Division.

A further long refit on the Tyne to Stage 2 condition 8.42 to 12.42, and a Tobermory workup, preceded a round trip to Gibraltar in the follow up to the North African invasion. The minelaying task declining rapidly after her return to the Kyle of Lochalsh, NEWARK had a two month refit at Newport, Mon. in 8.43 and 9.43 and then joined Rosyth Command for East Coast duty for the rest of the war.

NEWARK paid off to reserve in 7.45, was handed over to BISCo 18.2.47 and broken up at Bo'ness later that year by P. & W. MacLellan Ltd.

In Stage 2 state, NEWARK shows her new bridge, 271 and 291 radars; probably in early 12.42 after her Tyne refit
Admiralty

Shown in an intermedate state of refit. she has 271 radar and centreline torpedo tubes, but retains the beam 4" guns and appears to lack close range AA armament   *Admiralty*

HMS NEWMARKET G 47 (ex USS ROBINSON, DD 88)

NEWMARKET was handed over into Canadian custody at Halifax 26.11.40, and commissioned into the Royal Navy 5.12, when her crew arrived from the UK. In collision with NEWARK while en route, she eventually left Canadian waters after repair on 15.1.41 and commenced refit at Devonport 30.1. Apparently more work was required than the Dockyard could handle at that time, for on 5.2 she departed to the Humber where she remained under refit until 24.4.

After a very brief period of North Atlantic escort duty, NEWMARKET was taken in hand at Sheerness for further work from late 6 to 11.41, joining 8th Escort Group at Londonderry on completion. Here she was in collision with *GRENAA* on 6.12; and was obliged to leave convoy ON52 with boiler defects on 3.1.42. Repairs for both incidents, which took place at Londonderry and Liverpool, lasted until the end of 3.42, when NEWMARKET completed a round trip to Iceland with the first stage of convoy PQ14.

A survey of the ship in 5.42, after almost no front line service, showed her to be fit for Air Target duties only and she was therefore refitted at Rosyth 5.42 to 7.42, and thereafter employed within Rosyth Command. Even now she had problems, being laid up ineffective for eleven months from 7.43.

One of the least successful of the class, she paid off 1.7.45 and arrived at Llanelly 21.9 to be broken up by Rees Shipbreaking Co. Ltd.

HMS NEWPORT G 54 (ex USS SIGOURNEY, DD 81)

Delivered to the Canadians at Halifax 26.11.40, NEWPORT commissioned on 5.12 and arrived at Belfast en route to Devonport 30.12. Slightly damaged there in an air raid, she then broke down on passage south, and made temporary repairs at Milford Haven and later Cardiff, finally arriving at Devonport for refit 16.1.41, a refit that lasted until 24.9.

Manned by the Royal Norwegian Navy on completion, she was allocated to 43rd Escort Group; however further defects caused four weeks repair at Liverpool from 23.10, after which she joined 7th Escort Group based on Liverpool.

Employed briefly in the North Atlantic, NEWPORT collided with BEVERLEY 25.3.42, repaired initially at Liverpool to 13.5, then at Devonport to 10.9, finally passing to Southampton where she completed repair 20.5.43. Her Norwegian crew left her, and she paid off, in 6.42 so that she finally completed repair as a Royal Navy ship.

By the time repair, including re-tubing her boilers, was complete, she was no longer required as an escort so joined Western Approaches Command as an Air Target Ship, transferring to Rosyth Command in 3.44. She finally paid off 4.7.45, and arrived at Granton 18.2.47 to be broken up by Malcolm Brechin.

Newport 3/42

NEWPORT is shown here in a very limited Stage 1 conversion, and wearing the Norwegian Ensign. The date on the photograph is not the date of taking — see page 91
see page 91
Admiralty

Almost unchanged from her pre war state, only the beam tubes have been removed from NIAGARA and a 12pdr shipped aft. She has the standard 1940 TOWN camouflage scheme applied during her Devonport refit in 12.40
Admiralty

NIAGARA after further refit. She is in an intermediate state, retaining the beam 4" guns but with centreline torpedo tubes and the after funnels shortened. No radar is yet fitted. From the relaxed state of the crew on the upper deck, the open forward hatch and no guns manned, presumably she was photographed in southern waters away from operations, certainly prior to 1.43 when 271 radar was fitted

courtesy K. Macpherson

HMCS NIAGARA I 57 (ex USS THATCHER, DD 162)

The Royal Canadian Navy commissioned NIAGARA at Halifax 26.9.40 and after some initial escort work locally from that port, she was sent to Devonport for refit, arriving 30.11. The work, trials and defects plus a Tobermory work up occupied her until 4.41, then joining 4th Escort Group based at Greenock, sailing with her first convoy (OB306) on 5.4.41.

On the formation of the Newfoundland Escort Force NIAGARA returned to Canadian waters and operated from St John's NF. On 28.8.41 she was involved in the capture of U570, which had surrendered to a RAF Hudson the previous day. A two-month refit at Halifax from 15.9 preceded her return to North Atlantic escort; but the ship received weather damage 12.1.42 while escorting *TRITON* (also weather damaged) and in consequence she had to repair on the Clyde from 14.1.42 to 10.2.42, prior to returning to Halifax to join WLEF. Here she was involved in two rescues; survivors from the wrecked American *INDEPENDENCE HALL* on 9.3 off Sable Island, and recovering two boats from *RIO BLANCO* in 4.42.

As in so many TOWNs, boiler defects intervened and kept the ship in Halifax during 5 to 7.42, after which she resumed WLEF duties. In 5.43 she became part of unit W2, but increasing defects restricted her activities more and more as time passed. Finally, in 1.44, the RCN decided to limit her service to that of torpedo training ship based at Halifax, and she saw out the rest of her service there, being listed for disposal 15.9.45, placed on the sale list 27.5.46 and finally broken up at the end of 1947.

HMS RAMSEY G 60 (ex USS MEADE, DD 274)

RAMSEY commissioned at Halifax 26.11.40, sailed 5.12 and arrived for refit at Devonport 17.12, finally completing for service 29.1.41. After trials she joined 5th Escort Group based at Liverpool and worked from there until an engine breakdown 9.3 which required repairs lasting to 5.4. RAMSEY then continued with local escort work until transferred to the new NEF ariving St John's NF 11.6.41. In 8.41 she joined 22nd Escort Group, remaining part of it for a year during which she refitted at Boston from 11.41 to 2.42, and had major turbine repairs at Halifax and later Charleston SC from 5.4.42 to 24.7.42. Further work being required, RAMSEY took passage with convoy HX200 to Liverpool where repairs there, at Belfast and the Clyde took from 7.8 to 22.10.42.

Post refit, RAMSEY joined B6 Escort Group for one round trip, but then paid off for a long refit at Grimsby from 11.42 to 7.43. During this she received a new bridge and had major boiler repairs, but on completion of her post refit work up at Tobermory she was relegated to Air Target Ship in the Irish Sea.

RAMSEY paid off in 7.45 and laid up at Grangemouth, passing to BISCo 18.2.47 and being broken up at Bo'ness by P. & W. MacLellan Ltd in 7.47.

Probably taken post refit at Boston in 2.42. Although now fitted with 271 radar and centreline torpedo tubes, RAMSEY retains the minimal upper bridge and beam 4" guns, neither does she appear to mount any close range AA armament. The early, rotating, 286 radar aerial is very prominent in this photograph
USN

An early photograph of READING, which has a somewhat unusual appearance even for a TOWN. There is no upper bridge, the position is occupied by two 0.5" machine guns, the after funnels have yet to be shortened although a 12pdr has been mounted aft and the after tubes and mainmast removed. The overloading of the ship, even at this early date, can be seen by the partially submerged scuttles of the forward messdecks
Admiralty

HMS READING G 71 (ex USS BAILEY, DD 269)

Handed over at Halifax 26.11.40, READING arrived at Devonport 17.12 and completed trials and defects on 8.3.41. Based at Liverpool, READING escorted two convoys before arriving at Liverpool 3.4 with defects that required repair there until 11.5, after which she joined 8th Escort Group.

READING escorted four more convoys before transferring to NEF, arriving at St John's NF 7.7 and joining 23rd Escort Group there. Thereafter she was employed only briefly before returning to Londonderry with defects 2.5.42 and proceeding to London for long refit until 25.11.

READING worked up in the Cromarty Firth for five weeks after refit before becoming an Air Target Ship based in the Moray Firth. Remaining in that area, command transferred from Western Approaches to Rosyth in 2.44 and the ship finally paid off at Grangemouth 11.7.45. Sold 24.7.45, READING was broken up at Inverkeithing by T. W. Ward Ltd.

Photographed late in the war, RICHMOND here sports a new bridge, Hedgehog and 271 radar, centreline torpedo tubes and HF/DF on the pole mast aft. Single 20 mm are in the beam 4" gun positions, with two more aft on the searchlight bandstand.
Admiralty

HMS RICHMOND G 88 (ex USS FAIRFAX, DD 93)

The RCN took custody of RICHMOND at Halifax 26.11.40, and she commissioned 5.12 when her RN crew arrived, sailing for Devonport and refit 19.12. Delayed at St John's NF by defects, she arrived at Devonport 1.2.41; although completed and worked up by 16.3, a grounding at Holyhead while en route to Liverpool returned the ship for further repair at Southampton.

RICHMOND was allocated to NEF with 17th Escort Group when repairs were completed in early 6.41, escorting convoy WS9A for its first three days en route. Thereafter the ship was based at St John's NF until returning to Cardiff for a long refit starting 29.10.41. On completion of a Tobermory work up, RICHMOND joined 27th Escort Group based on the Clyde, her first task being to escort the initial stage PQ14 from the UK to Iceland, during which she collided with the American *FRANCIS SCOTT KEYS*. Damage was severe and, after being towed to Iceland for temporary repairs, she had then to be towed to Liverpool for repair.

When damage had been made good, and after a further work up, RICHMOND was ordered to join the WLEF, arriving at Halifax 1.9.42. In 2.43 she was again in collision, with REINHOLT, and again repaired at Liverpool 18.2 to 31.5.43, prior to returning to Canada. RICHMOND continued to be based at Halifax until 12.43, when she returned to Britain via Horta, arriving on the Tyne to lay up 27.12.43.

Allocated to Russia in lieu of Italian tonnage, she was refitted by Palmers, who were similarly refitting CHELSEA, and became ZHIVUCHI on 16.7.44 and passed to Kola for service with the Northern Fleet. She remained in Russian hands until 24.6.49 when she was returned to the RN at Rosyth, arriving at Grangemouth 29.7.49 to be broken up by G. & W. Brunton.

ZHIVUCHI at sea towing a torpedo target, probably post war from the clean state of paintwork, pennant etc.
courtesy Naval Museum, Leningrad

RICHMOND, the aftermath of the collision with FRANCIS SCOTT KEYS on 31.3.42. Taken prior to final repair, the temporary strengthening can be seen on the iron deck, also the exposed boiler

courtesy Naval Historical Branch

HMS RIPLEY entering harbour in late 1943, probably from post refit trials. The photograph clearly shows the Hedgehog fitted forward of the reconstructed bridge, 271 lantern above the bridge, and the newly fitted mainmast with HF/DF aerial   *Admiralty*

HMS RIPLEY G 79 (ex USS SHUBRICK, DD 268)

RIPLEY commissioned 26.11.40 at Halifax, and arrived at Devonport for refit 27.12. On completion on 13.2.41, she was in collision with BURWELL and the trawler NOTRE DAME DE FRANCE, which required further repairs until 3.3, followed at once by a patrol searching for a possible blockade runner.

Joining 5th Escort Group at Liverpool, RIPLEY commenced North Atlantic escort work with convoy OB308 on 6.4, and continued in that role until 8.41 only interrupted by acting as an A/S screen at Placentia Bay for PRINCE OF WALES and involvement in the BISMARCK search operations. Returning to Britain for refit with convoy TC12B, she was en route to Middlesbrough when she went ashore at Flamborough Head on 4.9. Towed off the same day, she had temporary repairs at Grimsby until 25.9, and then a protracted refit at Middlesbrough until 15.3.42.

After a seven day work up at Tobermory, RIPLEY covered the initial passage of convoy WS20 and then joined B2 Escort Group. Transferred to B7 Group early in 8.42, RIPLEY took convoy ON117 to Canada, and then went south with her Group to the Caribbean for duty with the USN there. Apparently found unsuitable, she returned to Halifax after one round trip, and to Britain with convoy SC103, arriving at Holyhead with defects 14.10. Temporarily repaired there, a long refit followed at Liverpool until 19.5.43, after which the ship was allocated to Admiral Commanding Orkney & Shetland for local duty. She worked up at Tobermory in 6.43, took part in Operation GOVERNOR in 7.43, and covered a troop convoy to the Faeroes in 8.43. Thereafter her duties were entirely local until she paid off to reserve on the Tyne arriving there 4.1.44. Transferred to BISCo 10.3.45, she arrived at Sunderland 14.4 to be broken up by Thos Young & Sons (Shipbreakers) Ltd.

This much earlier photograph of RIPLEY is in stark contrast to the previous, superb, print. Taken shortly after transfer and prior to major appearance changes, it nevertheless shows 286 radar with a fixed aerial, on the foremast; this dates it to 4 or 5.41   *courtesy K. Macpherson*

A superb picture of RIPLEY immaculate, probably after her refit in 3.42. Clearly shows the Hedgehog, a new bridge, 271 radar, capped forefunnel, searchlight moved to between funnels 2 and 3 with single 20 mm abeam, in the former searchlight bandstand, centreline torpedo tubes and HF/DF on the tall pole mast aft.
Admiralty

Another excellent view of RIPLEY clearly showing her new HF/DF mast and aerial and the general arrangements aft. One of a series of pictures of which three appear in the book
Admiralty

ROCKINGHAM, in 1942 probably at Liverpool immediately following her London refit   Admiralty

HMS ROCKINGHAM G 58 (ex USS SWASEY, DD 273)

Another late comer to the RN, ROCKINGHAM arrived at Devonport to refit 22.12.40, completing 22.2.41 to join 8th Escort Group. Local work in Western Approaches continued until 14.5.41, when increasing defects required a refit at Southampton during which the Stage 2 alterations were carried out, completing 21.8.

Returning to 8th EG, ROCKINGHAM escorted convoy OG74 outward on 13.9 and continued with normal convoy work until 12.41. On Christmas Eve she sailed with convoy CT8 from UK to Canada, returning with another troop convoy, NA1. Further special escort duty followed, convoy CT10 to Canada, the escort of armed merchant cruiser AUSONIA to Bermuda from Halifax and return in 2.42, and back to the UK with convoy NA4. ROCKINGHAM completed this spell of special duty by covering part of the first leg of convoy WS17 at the end of 3.42, then reverted to normal trade convoys until going to London for refit on 23.6.42.

Completing refit and work up in mid 11.42, ROCKINGHAM commenced escort work by bringing home convoy MKF1 from the North African invasion, then resumed trade convoy protection until 8.43 when she refitted at Belfast until mid 12.43 as an Air Target Ship. ROCKINGHAM worked up at Tobermory until 11.1.44 and was then allocated to Rosyth Command to serve the Eastern Scotland air stations.

On 27.9.44 while returning to Aberdeen, poor navigation brought her into the defensive minefields off the East coast, and after striking a mine she was abandoned and sank with the loss of one life.

ROCKINGHAM photographed in 1944 when serving as an Air Target Ship; the vertical lines on the hull are aiming marks for the trainee pilots. From the cluster of ratings forward of the bridge, the Hedgehog has been removed, otherwise she does not seem greatly altered from her escort days when seen from this angle
Admiralty

The censor passed this picture of ROXBOROUGH — subject to deletion of background and pennant number — on 31.1.41. It is one of a series taken during the Devonport refit and shows the "Devonport camouflage", and the U.S. 3"/23 calibre gun is still mounted between the forward 4" and the splinter mat-protected bridge. Her funnels have not yet been shortened either
Admiralty

Taken at the same time as the photograph on the previous page, this view of ROXBOROUGH shows the very similar starboard side camouflage, the removal of the after torpedo tubes and her sheeted armament. It makes an interesting contrast with the picture below, showing her appearance after her Charleston S.C. refit. Again the censor has marked the background and pennant number for blocking out Admiralty

HMS ROXBOROUGH I 07 (ex USS FOOTE, DD 169)

ROXBOROUGH commissioned 23.9.40 and sailed for Britain and refit 29.9, being obliged by defects to return to Halifax on 10.10. Repaired, she sailed again 7.12 and commenced refit on arrival at Devonport 27.12, completing 18.3.41 when she joined 2nd Escort Group, her first convoy being OB305 on 3.4. Transferred to 4th EG in 6.41, she was taken in hand for refit on the Clyde from 27.7 to 22.9.

Transferring to WLEF at Halifax, ROXBOROUGH took out convoy ON47 on 16.12. In need of repair on arrival she went south to Charleston SC for refit 12.1.42 to 26.3, and then returned to Halifax.

Grounding off Chebogue 24.6.42, ROXBOROUGH repaired at Norfolk Va until 9.9 before resuming her WLEF duties. In 1.43, while with convoy HX222 she met such heavy weather that the entire bridge structure was stove in with eleven dead and many injured; the dead included both Commanding Officer and 1st Lieutenant, the ship being handled thereafter by the sole surviving executive officer, a young RCNVR who happened to be aft at the time of damage. This Officer managed to regain control of the ship, and under hand steering from aft, she made St John's NF. Further repairs were made at Charleston SC, and it was not until 15.4.43 that she was able to resume duty at Halifax.

When, with other TOWNs of WLEF, ROXBOROUGH was released from duty, she sailed from St John's 31.12.,43 and arrived 10.1.44 on the Tyne to lay up. She was recommissioned and transferred to Russia as DOBLESTNYI on 10.8.44 and went to Kola to serve with the Russian Northern Fleet. Returning to Britain at Rosyth 7.2.49, she passed to BISCo 5.4 and arrived at Dunston on Tyne 14.5.49 to be broken up by Clayton & Davie Ltd.

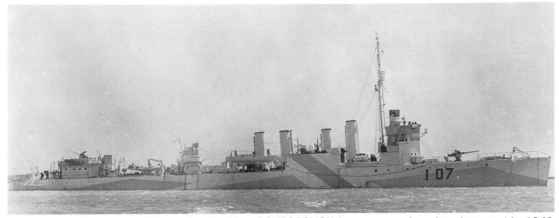

Another nice illustration of Stage 2 refit. Here ROXBOROUGH is seen out of an American yard in 1943. Hedgehog has yet to be fitted forward, but the bridge has been reconstructed. 20 mm can be seen abeam the funnels and the searchlight tower, with the centreline torpedo tubes just abaft it. She is also fitted with 291 radar USN

ST. ALBANS in 5.42; she has 271 radar as well as 291, but retains the beam 4" guns. No torpedo tubes seem to be fitted, while the US 3"/23 calibre gun mounted between A gun and the bridge has been retained for some odd reason   *Admiralty*

HMS ST ALBANS I 15 (ex USS THOMAS, DD 182)

Commissioned at Halifax 23.9.40, ST ALBANS refitted at Devonport, from 11.10 to 1.11 and then joined the 1st Minelaying Squadron at the Kyle of Lochalsh base. From here she escorted minelaying sorties, and the initial days of convoys WS4B and WS5A, prior to refitting at Chatham 11.2 to 22.4.41. On 14.4 she was transferred to the Royal Norwegian Navy for manning.

Collision with (and the sinking of) the minesweeping trawler ALBERIC on 3.5 during her work up, delayed the ship's return to duty until 4.6 when she joined 7th Escort Group based at Liverpool. On 18.6 she picked up survivors from *EMPIRE DEW*, and while with convoy SC 81 took part in the sinking of U401 on 3.8. Damaged while with convoy ON22 on 7.10, she was partly repaired in Iceland, and then in London for a further six weeks completing in mid 12.41.

Returning to her old Group, ST ALBANS fitted 271 radar in Liverpool in 3.42, then followed this with a return convoy passage to Iceland and convoy PQ15 to Russia. During this passage, she encountered the Polish submarine JASTRZAB well off station and, in company with SEAGULL, attacked and sank it. ST ALBANS returned to Britain with convoy QP12 and then went to Falmouth for refit from 5.7.

During this refit, ST ALBANS reverted to British manning, completed refit 29.10 and worked up at Tobermory to 8.11. Her first convoy was ON144 from which she returned with defects, arriving at Devonport 16.11 and repairing there, and at Portsmouth, until the end of the year. ST ALBANS then did temporary duty with Rosyth Command as a Target Ship and rectified defects at Devonport before sailing with convoy ON177 to join WLEF at Halifax, where she served until 12.43.

Returning to Britain to go into reserve with the other WLEF TOWNs, ST ALBANS was transferred to Russia 16.7.44 as DOSTOINYI following a refit at Palmers from 2.6 to 22.6.44. She served with the Northern Fleet based on Kola, and returned to Britain being handed over at Rosyth 28.2.49. Passed to BISCo 5.4, she was towed away to Charlestown 18.5 to be broken up by Metal Industries Ltd.

A later view of ST. ALBANS, still flyng the Norwegian ensign, but with a new bridge, beam 4" replaced by 20 mm Oerlikon, two new centreline mountings of 20 mm Oerlikons abaft the fourth funnel and the searchlight replaced by a final pair of 20 mm Oerlikons. She now mounts triple torpedo tubes in the after position. The mast raking forward at the stern belongs to a lighter lying alongside   *Admiralty*

ST CLAIR shown very early in Canadian service, the only alterations being the removal of the mainmast and after torpedo tubes, even the after 4" gun is still mounted, dating the photograph to 10 or 11.40
      Admiralty

HMCS ST CLAIR I 65 (ex USS WILLIAMS, DD 108)

One of the six initial Canadian ships, ST CLAIR commissioned at Halifax 24.9.40 and served as a local escort. She steamed to Britain as part of the escort for convoy HX91 and arrived on the Clyde 11.12; unusually her refit started there and the ship did not transfer to Devonport until 12.1, completing 17.3.41.

After working, up ST CLAIR escorted the first stage of convoy WS7 and then joined 4th Escort Group for Western Approaches work. During the hunt for BISMARCK she was diverted to search duties and was with MASHONA when the latter was sunk 27.5 by air attack, rescuing survivors with TARTAR.

Returning to Canada with convoy OB328 in 5.41, ST CLAIR arrived at St John's NF 7.6 and, shortly afterwards, collided with the station tanker *CLAM* moored in the harbour, necessitating repair at Halifax and St John's from 23.6 to 10.11.41. She then started escort work with WLEF, rescuing survivors from *NYHOLT* on 27.1.42.

ST CLAIR remained a Halifax based escort, albeit with increasing defect time, until 1.44 when, replaced by modern ships, she became depot ship at Halifax for submarines based there for A/S training. In 8.44 she paid off from that duty and became a static hulk for the Damage Control School, being finally declared redundant and sold for scrap 5.3.46.

Taken in 1942, this picture of ST CROIX illustrates very well the partial alterations to the Canadian ships vis a vis their British counterparts. While centreline torpedo tubes have now been mounted aft, the beam 4" guns are retained, the bridge remains unaltered, there appears to be no close range AA armament and the only radar is SW1C
courtesy K. Macpherson

HMCS ST CROIX I 81 (ex USS McCOOK, DD 252)

Alone of the Canadian TOWNs, ST CROIX had an active, oceanic career and one of the saddest ends for a Canadian warship. ST CROIX commissioned at Halifax 24.9.40 and initially served as a local escort, refitting there in late 10/11.40 prior to departing to Britain and long refit. Suffering weather damage on the way, she finally made St John's NF after a search had started, and she returned to Halifax for repairs lasting to mid 3.41. In consequence, she never came to Britain for refit as intended but remained in Canadian waters, with NEF and then 21st Escort Group.

Her first major refit was at St John's NF from 9.41 to 4.42, after which she took up duty with MOEF. While with convoy ON113 she attacked and sank U90 on 24.7.42, the high spot of that year prior to refit at St John's for five weeks in 11 and 12.42.

Sent to Britain with convoy HX222 in 1.43, ST CROIX worked up at Tobermory 22.1 to 17.2 as part of the intensive effort to remedy training defects in the RCN escort fleet; a policy that paid off on 4.3.43 when, as part of the escort for convoy KMS10, ST CROIX and SHEDIAC sank U87. Returning from North Africa with MKS9, ST CROIX returned to the North Atlantic and Halifax for repair in 6 and 7.43.

In 8.43, ST CROIX transferred to Britain again to join in the Bay of Biscay A/S offensive, and she became involved in the intense actions that developed around the combined convoys ON202 and ONS18 on 19.9.43 during which the Germans deployed the acoustic torpedo with some success. Twice torpedoed by U305 on 20.9, ST CROIX sank and her survivors were taken on board the frigate ITCHEN, their misfortune being that this ship in turn was lost in the continuing action on 22.9, with very heavy loss of life. From the two sinkings, only one of ST CROIX's crew of 147 survived.

In this photograph, ST FRANCIS shows basic alterations, the mainmast reduced to a stump, shortened funnels, a modified bridge, 286 radar and the usual 12pdr aft and the loss of the after tubes　　　　　*Admiralty*

HMCS ST FRANCIS I 93 (ex USS BANCROFT, DD 256)

Commissioned into the Royal Canadian Navy at Halifax 24.9.40, ST FRANCIS served as a local escort until 1.41 when she arrived on the Clyde for refit and subsequent work up at Tobermory, finally completing in early 4.41 to join 4th Escort Group, with which she served until mid 7.41 when she went to Pictou for refit. During the intervening period she escorted a number of convoys, and rescued the crew of *STARCROSS* on 20.5.

During the Pictou refit, the after boiler and funnel were removed to provide an increased bunker capacity of 470 tons, and she also had her bridge rebuilt. It is not clear if the choice of No 4 boiler was dictated by damage, as in ANNAPOLIS, or by the experience gained from that ship's alterations. The USN also removed No 4 boiler in some ships for a similar reason, whereas the RN in their three TOWN conversions favoured the forward boilers.

Below, the picture tells a different story. Single 20 mm have replaced the beam 4" guns, the bridge has been totally rebuilt, 271 radar fitted, all torpedo tubes removed and, most obvious of all, the third funnel. It appears that No 3 boiler has gone in a like manner to ANNAPOLIS, to provide additional fuel storage to increase the range of the ship　　　　　*courtesy K. Macpherson*

Joining NEF on completion of refit in 10.41, ST FRANCIS was widely employed in the North Atlantic, refitting at Londonderry mid 9 to mid 11.42 and at Halifax 5.12.42 to 16.4.43. In 4.43 she joined C2 Group for a brief period, and then repaired at Halifax in 7.43 after which she joined 9th Escort Group and then WEF.

Taken in hand with defects at Shelburne in late 10.43, she was surveyed and assigned as static depot ship to CORNWALLIS shore establishment in 2.44, in which capacity she remained until 1.4.45 when she was turned over to the Crown War Assets Disposal Commission. Sold to Frankel Bros for breaking up, she was wrecked in tow after a collision with *WINDING GULF* on 14.7.45, while en route to the breaker's yard. Her consort on that occasion was HAMILTON; some reports indicate that it may have been that ship which was lost, certainly one flush decker lies wrecked as a result of the incident.

This photograph, taken from a print purchased onboard ST MARYS by a member of her crew, is in fact a fake; a fact only becoming apparent after its selection for the book. In reality, it is a photograph of MANSFIELD under the Norwegian ensign, with the relevant pennant number obliterated
A good example of the problems inherent in wartime photographs even when their provenance appears undoubted
courtesy W. Wood Esq

The author will welcome any authenticated photograph of ST MARYS, the only ship not illustrated in this work

HMS ST MARYS I 12 (ex USS DORAN ex USS BAGLEY, DD 185)

This ship was struck from the register of the USN years prior to her transfer to Britain and, like LEWES, had to assume a different name when recommissioned by the USN as the original one had been re-used for new construction. She finally became ST MARYS on 23.9.40.

Sailing on 29.9, ST MARYS had the briefest of refits at Devonport 14.10 to 1.11, and then joined the 1st Minelaying Squadron at Kyle of Lochalsh becoming involved in some of the first sorties made. Her service with the Squadron was to continue, other than for refits, until mid 1943.

Having had so short an initial refit, it is not surprising that ST MARYS went into dockyard hands in 12.40 for two months, not again needing repair apparently until 1.9.41 after a collision with *ROYAL ULSTERMAN* in convoy SD10, the damage keeping her at Liverpool until 15.12.41.

Considering her employment in northern waters, and her age, it is surprising that her next major repair was not until 12.42, and that after going aground at Lerwick and remaining fast for three days. Repairs, at Leith, took until 17.2.43 followed by a work up at Tobermory until 3.3 prior to returning to Kyle of Lochalsh for the final operations of the Minelaying Squadron before disbanding. ST MARYS then passed to Rosyth Command for East Coast duty.

Age beginning to take its toll, ST MARYS refitted at Newport, Mon. commencing 6.11.43, but the work was delayed and finally cancelled with the ship being paid off to reserve on the Tyne on 23.2.44. Approved for disposal in 9.44, she was passed to BISCo 20.3.45 and finally arrived at Rosyth in 12.45 to be broken up by Metal Industries Ltd.

For a ship completed in 8.19, that had lain idle from 7.22 until 6.40 and which had been officially discarded in 1935, ST MARYS set a remarkable record for remaining in wartime service.

The photographs, above and below, show SALISBURY with the usual 1942 alterations: 271 radar, centreline torpedo tubes aft, HF/DF and 20 mm Oerlikons in the beam positions and further aft. No Hedgehog is fitted, which dates the photographs to between 6 and 8.42   Admiralty

HMS SALISBURY I 52 (ex USS CLAXTON, DD 140)

Not commissioned at Halifax until 5.12.40, SALISBURY arrived at Devonport 9.1.41 for a refit lasting until 3.3. Thereafter the ship worked up in the Channel prior to joining 2nd Escort Group for the North Atlantic. Transferring later to 4th EG, SALISBURY worked up until 26.10.41 when she arrived at Rosyth for further refit and alteration.

On completion of refit, SALISBURY was employed as a special escort for specific convoys, including several of the WS series of troop convoys, the return of the US carrier WASP from Operation CALENDAR and the subsequent passage of the same ship to Gibraltar for Operation BOWERY (both operations being the supply of Spitfires to Malta, flown off from WASP).

In 9.42, SALISBURY went to Halifax and joined WLEF, she needed major boiler repair shortly after and went to Charleston SC from late 11.42 to mid 1.43, and had a further lengthy spell at Boston 6.4.43 to 12.6.43.

Returning to duty at Halifax with WLEF, SALISBURY finally paid off due to defects and laid up at Halifax 10.12.43. She was offered to the USN as a source of spares for their flush deckers, but the offer was declined and she was listed for disposal 22.4.44 and sold 26.6, eventually being broken up in the USA during 4.45.

Not the best of photographs, but the only one located. Taken fairly late in the war with the usual Stage 2 alterations, SHERWOOD seems to have a problem as she is stopped (or almost so) rolling in a moderate sea and with the 'Not under control' signal flying
Admiralty

HMS SHERWOOD I 80 (ex USS RODGERS, DD 254)

Commissioned at Halifax 23.10.40, SHERWOOD sailed for Britain 1.11 being delayed both by a search for JERVIS BAY survivors and having to return with defects to St John's NF, where she arrived 7.11. Sailing again on 12.11, she arrived at Portsmouth to refit 26.11, one of the few ships not to be taken in hand at Devonport. Damaged in an air raid by a near miss 11.3.41, she transferred to Devonport to complete, this being done by 8.4, and then joined 12th Escort Group based in Iceland. From that base, SHERWOOD escorted Atlantic convoys in their mid passage, took part in the search for BISMARCK, and, with ST CLAIR, supported TARTAR after the sinking of MASHONA at the end of that search.

Allocated to NEF in 7.41, SHERWOOD instead had to refit on the Clyde for two months, joining 2nd Escort Group at Londonderry on completion. After escorting only two convoys, SHERWOOD transferred to 22nd EG in 11.41 until sustaining weather damage 27.1.42. Repaired after a brief period, SHERWOOD escorted FORMIDABLE and then ILLUSTRIOUS during sea trials in 2 and 3.42, after which she needed further work including retubing her boilers, work which lasted at Liverpool until 25.8.42.

Completing repair and the subsequent work up, SHERWOOD was temporarily employed as an Air Target Ship in the Cromarty area until mid 10.42, when she went to St John's NF to join MOEF. In 3.43 she became part of C2 Group, and made a return passage from the UK to North Africa, on completion of which she was laid up at Londonderry, defective.

After being surveyed in 4.43, it was decided that SHERWOOD was beyond economic repair, and she was transferred to Chatham and stripped of usable parts for her sisters. On 28.9.43, in tow of the tug *SEA GIANT*, she left Chatham and joined convoy FN1640 in tow for the Humber. On 30.9 she was formally removed from the effective list, being beached on 3.10.43 in position 58.37.07N 00.05.05W in the Humber Approaches and used as a target for RAF rocket equipped Beaufighters. The wreck was, eventually, dispersed under the RN wreck dispersal programme post war.

Taken shortly after an air raid on Devonport 28/29.4.41, the interest in this picture lies in the stripped hulk in the foreground which is in fact STANLEY in the later stages of her conversion to a Long Range Escort. The old fashioned anchor and the shield of A gun are the tell tales, other than the pennant of course. The base of the new bridge structure can be seen, presumably the stripping out of the boiler rooms has already been done in dry dock
Admiralty

HMS STANLEY I 73 (ex USS McCALLA, DD 253)

STANLEY's RN career commenced somewhat inauspiciously when defects forced her to return to St John's NF during her initial passage. Repairs at St John's delayed her from 6.11 to 13.12.40, and she did not finally make Devonport until 2.1.41, having been further delayed at Belfast.

Once taken in hand at Devonport, it was decided that the scale of work needed was such as to justify her inclusion with BRADFORD and CLARE in the first Long Range Escort programme. Accordingly she was gutted amidships with the two forward boilers being replaced with bunkers and stores, etc, a new bridge structure extended aft to the two after funnels, and she was fitted with 271 radar and centreline torpedo tubes. When completed in 9.41 she was one of the more potent A/S escorts available.

Because of her increased range, STANLEY was allocated initially to the Liverpool Sloop Division to escort convoys on the OS/SL cycles to and from Sierra Leone. She then transferred to the 40th Escort Group where she came under the command of Captain Walker, who was to make his name as the pre-eminent submarine hunter of the war.

STANLEY is shown above on completion of her conversion to a Long Range Escort at Devonport. 271 radar tops her new bridge, there are 20 mm Oerlikon in the beam positions, and centreline tubes aft
Admiralty

With 40th EG and under Captain Walker's overall command, STANLEY was one of the escorts for convoy HG76 from Gibraltar, the first convoy to have a properly organised and trained Escort Group and Escort Carrier with it, and the first to be fought through against a concerted submarine attack by such a combination. In the confused fighting around the convoy from 17 to 19.12.41, STANLEY and her consorts sank U131 on 17.12, and U434 on 18.12. STANLEY was lost to U574 on 19.12 with the loss of all but 25 of her crew. Revenge was immediate, U574 being sunk by STORK within minutes of STANLEY's loss.

Brief though STANLEY's career was, she demonstrated both the validity of the Long Range Escort concept, and also the effectiveness of a properly trained and led Escort Group with carrier support.

HMS WELLS I 95 (ex USS TILLMAN, DD 135)

Alphabetically the last of the TOWNs, WELLS was also amongst the last to commission, on 5.12.40. Unfortunately, she collided with both NEWMARKET and a jetty on 9.12, so that her sailing for the UK was delayed until 17.12, and defects delayed her at St John's NF until 30.1.41. She then returned to Halifax for repairs, and sailed for Britain on 4.2, only to be towed back by NEWARK the same day. Further repairs at Halifax and, later, St John's ensued so that it was not until 9.3 that WELLS arrived at Devonport for her refit, which completed on 10.4.

WELLS joined the 1st Minelaying Squadron at Kyle of Lochalsh, arriving there 13.4.41. However, her major involvement was on loan as an escort to the Icelandic ferry convoy system, and she covered sixteen of these convoys and only five minelaying sorties before going to refit on the Humber on 3.9.41.

The Humber refit lasted until 25.11, followed by a weeks work up at Tobermory before returning to Kyle of Lochalsh. This time, rather more escort work for the minelayers was involved, though WELLS still found her attention claimed by the Icelandic convoys as well. A further refit commenced, this time at Newport, Mon, in 6.42 during which she finally received 271 radar.

The Newport refit and subsequent work up at Tobermory completed in mid 9.42, and WELLS completed the year with a varied selection of duties including escorting *QUEEN MARY,* Icelandic convoys, minelaying sorties and a return convoy to North Africa after Operation TORCH. Not surprisingly, a month's refit was needed after this strenuous programme, carried out on the Clyde during 1.43. Following this, WELLS returned to the Minelaying Squadron for its closing phase in early 1943, and then went again to Newport Mon. on 6.4 for further repair.

A late war photograph of WELLS very probably during her service on the East Coast prior to 10.44
Admiralty

On completion of a two weeks Tobermory work up, WELLS came under the command of the Home Fleet on 1.8.43; after a brief period she and her sisters from the former minelayer escort then passed to Rosyth for duty on the East Coast. WELLS herself had a month in dockyard hands, both for defects and to fit the specialised equipment needed (VHF etc), and then spent a year working with the convoys between Rosyth and Harwich. In 10.44 Rosyth dockyard spent six weeks stripping the old ship and preparing her for a new role as an Air Target Ship, the work completing 26.11.44. WELLS transferred to the Clyde, but defects intervened and she did not actually commence work as a target until mid 4.45, and the end of the war caused her to pay off and transfer to BISCo on 24.7. WELLS arrived at Troon in 2.46 to be broken up by West of Scotland Shipbreaking Co Ltd.

"Make Smoke!" WELLS seems to be posing for the photographer in this 1942 photograph   *Admiralty*

Convoy scene: Convoy HX118 photographed between 10.4 and 15.4.41 from RAMSEY, whose guns are to be seen on the left, and showing RIPLEY on the right. The censor requires RIPLEY's pennant number to be blocked out before the picture is released to the public
Admiralty

The battleship ROYAL SOVEREIGN, the submarines SUNFISH, URSULA, UNISON and UNBROKEN and two — unfortunately unidentified — TOWN class destroyers lying in the Dockyard Basin at Rosyth preparing for departure to Russia in 1944
Admiralty

Winter North Atlantic: LEAMINGTON at St. John's NF   *Admiralty*

INDEX TO SHIPS' HISTORIES AND PHOTOGRAPHS

The fifty ships which are the subject of this book. Names in Royal and Royal Canadian Navy service are printed in **bold** type, in United States Navy service in roman type and in Russian Navy service in *italic* type. Building details of all ships are given on pages 14 and 15; and commissioning dates at Halifax on page 18.

A splendidly clear starboard quarter view of NEWPORT flying the Norwegian ensign and probably taken shortly after completion of the Devonport refit in 11.41. It shows clearly the 286 radar which was omitted from the picture on page 67, also the unusual replacement of the beam torpedo tubes by a centreline mounting even though the beam 4" are still mounted   *Admiralty*

THE LAST AT SEA

The former HMS LEAMINGTON, returned after service with the Russian Northern Fleet and sold for breaking up, was chartered from the breakers and refurbished to serve as a 'prop' for the film THE GIFTHORSE based on the St Nazaire raid. Here she is seen in her temporary guise, superficially altered so as vaguely to resemble CAMPBELTOWN, entering Portsmouth Harbour as the last TOWN at sea under her own power.

This photograph, by courtesy of WSPL, was discovered by Richard Osborne in the course of cataloguing the Kennedy Collection. It was taken between 8 and 11.51. A fuller account of events regarding the ship can be found in MARINE NEWS, vol 5, page 124   World Ship Photo Library, Kennedy collection